MRS. GREENTHUMBS

PLOWS AHEAD

Mrs. Greenthumbs Plows Ahead

Five Steps to the Drop-Dead Gorgeous Garden of Your Dreams

Cassandra Danz

Illustrations by Barbara Maslen

CROWN PUBLISHERS, INC.
NEW YORK

Published by Crown Publishers, Inc., 201 East 50th Street, New York, New York 10022. Member of the Crown Publishing Group.

Random House, Inc. New York, Toronto, London, Sydney, Auckland
www.randomhouse.com/

CROWN and colophon are trademarks of Crown Publishers, Inc.

Printed in the United States of America

Design by Lauren Dong

Library of Congress Cataloging-in-Publication Data
Danz, Cassandra.
    Mrs. Greenthumbs plows ahead : five steps to the drop-dead
gorgeous garden of your dreams / Cassandra Danz. — 1st ed.
        p.   cm.
    Includes index.
    1. Landscape gardening.   2. Gardens—Design.   3. Landscape gardening—Philosophy.
    4. Gardens—Anecdotes.   5. Gardening—Anecdotes.   I. Title.
    SB473.D355   1998
    712'.6—dc21   97-30270
                                                           CIP

ISBN 0-517-70554-0

10   9   8   7   6   5   4   3   2

ACKNOWLEDGMENTS

MY GRATITUDE TO all the great gardeners I visited on my travels in the United States and England—Mary Keen, David Benner, Hugh Johnson, Phyllis Gustafson, Shirley Cargill, Anne Chambers, Wanda Fielder, and Christopher Lloyd.

Thanks to Ken Slevin, Peter Bevacqua, Michael Gelman, Pam Jones, Don Christensen, Mickey and George, Jim M., Charles Baker, Norman Posner, Pam Dubois, Sally McCabe and Janet Carter, Bob and Lydia, and the other gardeners and friends who populate the pages of this book.

Thanks to Katherine Powis of the New York Horticultural Society for her advice and help.

I would especially like to thank my dear pal Bobbie Gelman, and, as always, Ron Lackmann. Special thanks to Mary Fulham. And of course to Walter and Sam. And to my mother, always.

Contents

Acknowledgments   VII

Introduction   XV

Extreme Gardening   xvii

1. Create the Garden as a Separate Place Away from the World   1

The Cottage Garden   1
Garden Rooms   16
The Third Room   46
My First Christopher Lloyd Story   53

2. Plant Perennials and Plant Them Abundantly!   56

Abundance   57
Herbaceous Perennials, the Queens of the Garden   62

Shrubs, the Queens of the Perennial Garden 68

Trees, the Queens of the Perennial Garden 74

Proportion 81

Making Perennials, the Queens of the Garden, Do the Work 85

More Ways to Use Perennials 92

3. Use Plants That Grow Easily in Your Climate and Location 95

Where to Put Plantings in Relation to the House 97

East 99

North 100

West 104

South 105

How to Find the Best Plants for Your Garden 113

A Desert Garden 122

The Dearly Departed 124

Benign Negligence 125

The Hudson Valley Plant Sale 126

Reaping Mother Nature's Bounty 128

But Don't Use Plants That Are *Too* Easy to Grow 130

But Don't Use Plants That Are *Too* Hard to Grow 131

4. Have Something in Bloom Throughout the Gardening Season 133

Some Exceptions 134

The Most Beautiful Rose Garden I've Ever Seen 135

Climaxing 139

A Season of Climaxes 139

Planning a Long-Season Garden with Shrubs   143

You Should Have Seen It Last Week   146

Using Container Plants to Fill in Lulls   147

How to Keep the Garden Abundant and Everblooming   150

Composting for Everyone   151

How to Use Compost   153

Other *Mulchés!*   155

How to Use *Mulché!*   158

Instant *Mulché!*   159

The Day I Fell Off the Chemical Wagon   161

Weeding the Garden   165

Another Christopher Lloyd Story   167

5. DON'T PLANT MAGENTA NEXT TO TAXICAB YELLOW!   168

The Art of Color   169

Color Gardens   172

The White Garden   173

The Blue Garden   177

The Red Garden   179

The Yellow Garden   181

The Gray Garden   183

The Green Garden   185

Color Intensity as a Unifying Theme and Other Ways to Employ Color   187

My Color Madness   190

My Last Christopher Lloyd Story   191

INDEX   193

"Gardening is a humanizing occupation."

CHRISTOPHER LLOYD

INTRODUCTION

AFTER WRITING *Mrs. Greenthumbs: How I Turned a Boring Yard into a Glorious Garden and How You Can, Too,* I've had quite a few adventures. Under my *nom de voyage,* Mrs. Greenthumbs, I have traveled far and met many interesting people. I have also met many dull people, but I won't bore you with them. If I have to mention them at all, it will only be as supporting characters and I will try to make them seem as interesting as possible.

Through a series of miracles, I have had the opportunity to travel and meet some of the best gardeners in the United States and in England. Even better, I've been able to tour their gardens and ask questions about them.

The more gardens I saw, the more I came to realize that great gardens have many elements in common. From these elements I have distilled five essential steps to great gardening. I would venture to say that, if you apply these five principles, you can make a beautiful garden anywhere in the world.

Arguably, there are more than five steps to fine horticulture and everyone has a few of their own to add. Some say that weeding is most important, some composting. Respected garden writers like Ken Druse or Sara Stein suggest that we use only native plants and wildflowers. That's all very well, but this is my book and I think these five are the most important:

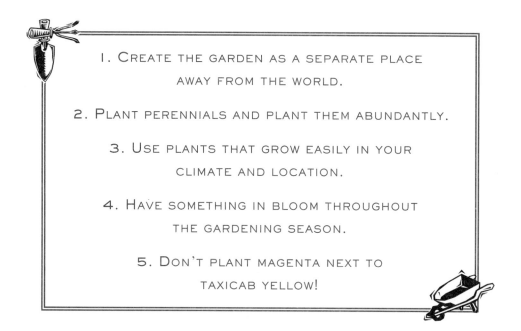

1. CREATE THE GARDEN AS A SEPARATE PLACE AWAY FROM THE WORLD.

2. PLANT PERENNIALS AND PLANT THEM ABUNDANTLY.

3. USE PLANTS THAT GROW EASILY IN YOUR CLIMATE AND LOCATION.

4. HAVE SOMETHING IN BLOOM THROUGHOUT THE GARDENING SEASON.

5. DON'T PLANT MAGENTA NEXT TO TAXICAB YELLOW!

Not all of the wonderful gardens I saw followed all of the five steps, especially the one about magenta and taxicab yellow. And the fourth step seems to be the hardest for everyone. Keeping the garden in bloom all season is a real challenge, especially for gardeners like David Benner, a Pennsylvania college professor with a shady woodland garden. Shade gardens bloom mostly in spring. Phyllis Gustafson, who has a rock garden in Oregon, doesn't really follow step three, since her pleasure is to grow plants that are rare and difficult.

Not one of these gardeners has a boring front lawn! Before I talk about my five principles of gardening, I would like to say a few words about my pet peeve.

I was tempted to set it down as a step: "Put something besides a lawn in your front yard, for heaven's sake!" Although it's true that there are places where grass is appropriate and necessary, most people mow down the whole front garden! Or rather, the garden that would be there if they didn't maul the landscape by chopping off everything over three inches high. I call this "Extreme Gardening."

EXTREME GARDENING

In *The Art of Beautifying Suburban Home Grounds*, published in 1870, landscape architect Frank J. Scott "envisioned our suburbs as private property unified by a flawless turf to form the visual equivalent of a great public park."* This view has been very appealing to twentieth-century Americans, a nation filled with democratic ideals and armed with power lawn mowers. Over the years, it has been adopted in every part of the country, and I needn't tell you how much the lawn-care products industry wants to keep it that way.

The truth is, however, suburban developments are not public parks. Can you imagine driving up to somebody's suburban front lawn, spreading a blanket, and having a picnic? You'd risk getting shot.

Children don't play in the front yard—the ball could roll into the street and the child might be hit by a car; you can't have a cocktail party out there because the neighbors would know they weren't invited; only an exhibitionist would sunbathe on his front lawn. For lack of hedges or fences, the front windows of most suburban homes look out right on the street. Who can get romantic when anyone passing by can look into the living room? (I suspect that this arrangement is responsible for the appalling statistic that 46 percent of American couples make love less than once a week.)

If you ask me, the whole front lawn concept is an invasion of privacy, and it makes Americans neurotic. On the one hand, we are told that to reveal our deepest emotions is therapeutic and "healthy." Don't put up walls, don't block the free flow of uninhibited, "honest" emotions, we are advised. Revealing the intimate details of one's life to strangers in airports, dentists' waiting rooms, and during media interviews and other public occasions is a common practice.

Full exposure may serve the person doing the confessing as some kind of cathartic release, but like most people I get very uncomfortable when someone I don't know starts "sharing" with me. I think most of us have our own problems and appreciate—no, long for—social boundaries to protect us.

But we also like to seem open and honest.

---

*Allen Lacy, "Home Turf," *New York Times Magazine*, October 15, 1989.

This ambivalence is reflected in our gardens. Because we want to appear to be open, we have no walls between our front yards, and as a result we never go out there. Have you ever seen anybody enjoying themselves on the front lawn? Or even not enjoying themselves? Have you ever seen anybody at all? Most of us hang out in the back of the house and we don't dare go near the front yard at all, except to be seen mowing it once a week.

In California, this is called a "boundary issue." The reason it's an issue is because there is no boundary. I say, the more defined the boundary, the less you have to fake being "open." With the lines clearly drawn, it is safe to be truly friendly, because everyone knows where to stop.

I have been accused of being too adamant about this front lawn business. "Get off it, Cassandra," people tell me. They say that they like lawns because they're so familiar and accessible.

Men tell me that they enjoy mowing the lawn on Saturday. It's the machinery. Sitting atop a satisfyingly loud riding mower, pulsing power between their legs, is much more fun than pulling weeds from flower beds, and more manly, too.

It does sound like fun, and I understand that a lot of guys love machines. I think there are much more mucho macho activities than lawn mowing, however, like lassoing woodchucks, erecting fences, coaching kids, or fighting fires. And what is more manly than making donations to blood banks or, even more virile, sperm banks?

I don't want to hit you over the head with this point, but I insist that we must abolish the dysfunctional (not to mention nonfunctional) front yards of the present, get rid of the boundaryless, chemically codependent front lawn, and take back the land and reclaim it as our own private space. Like so much of the inhabited world, we Americans need fences, hedges, and walls, not so much to keep other people out, but to make a lovely place away from the world for us to spend time in. This book is about creating that lovely place.

Mrs.

Greenthumbs

Plows Ahead

CREATE THE GARDEN AS A
SEPARATE PLACE
AWAY FROM THE WORLD

THE COTTAGE GARDEN

Every man's home may be his castle, but only metaphorically. Most American suburban homes, even those with five or six bedrooms, are cottages, no matter how high the property taxes. The average suburban lot is one-quarter to one-half acre. The compatible garden for such a site is an American cottage garden.

Traditionally, a cottage garden is one where trees, shrubs, and herbaceous cultivars all grow together informally. While cottage gardens are frequently enclosed by a fence or hedge, there are not too many clipped shrubs and strictly manicured plantings. Plants are allowed to grow through the picket fence and spill over the paths. While the actual plants may vary depending on the geographical location—roses and privet or cacti and tropical palms—the overall feeling of the cottage garden is healthy abundance of flowers and foliage.

This is Chatsworth, home of the Dukes of Devonshire in England. Notice the clipped shrubbery, the magnificent statuary, the lawns suitable for grazing sheep. Chatsworth.

This is the Chativitzkys' house. Note the clipped shrubbery, the magificent statuary, the lawn suitable for grazing sheep.

Chatsworths live in England. Chativitzkys live in Flushing, Queens. There is quite a difference between these two homes, yet the smaller dwelling is inappropriately landscaped in the style of the larger one.

Imagine how a suburban street would look if each tract house were landscaped like an American cottage rather than an English manor house. I often have that image in my mind's eye as I sit looking out the window while my husband, Walter, drives the old Ponti around the countryside. As we roll down the street, I see teeny-weeny Chatsworth landscapes, but I dream that they are American cottage gardens.

We pass a white and green-shuttered colonial house with two foundation shrubs and a postage-stamp lawn. We've all seen this arrangement a thousand times. But in that same moment, I see the yard enclosed by a white picket fence spilling over with flowers. Over the gate is an arch covered with an old rambler rose called the Seven Sisters because each rose in the cluster turns a different shade of pink as the blooms mature. Between the arch and the front door, there are plantings of peonies, phlox, tiger lilies, and flowering shrubs, all blooming at once. (This is a fantasy, remember?)

We pass a ranch house with two foundation shrubs and a slightly larger post office window lawn. I imagine an unpainted wooden fence behind a line of honey locust trees, which almost meet to form an arch over the driveway. In and around the fence, shrubs are planted from the corner of the house out toward the street, filling the yard with color and form.

We pass a split-level with two foundation shrubs and a disgruntled postal worker lawn. I imagine it surrounded by a split-rail fence enclosing native trees and a woodland garden with birdhouses tucked among the greenery. In spring it is filled with daffodils, in summer with ferns, and in fall it all turns gold and scarlet and smells fabulous. This garden requires almost no maintenance.

We pass a rusty pink and turquoise blue mobile home on cinder block pilings and seventeen pickup trucks of various ages in the middle of a two-acre lawn. I see the view improved by a twelve-foot stone wall. Or dynamite.

The way to begin to design a cottage garden appropriate to the American house and yard is to separate it visually, psychologically, or physically from the surrounding suburban "public park."

Walls

The most unequivocal way to separate the front yard is to build a wall around it. This total enclosure may not be for everyone, but an opaque, impenetrable wall made of stone, brick, stucco, or adobe that is six to eight feet high can be an architectural wonder. In rocky areas, garden walls are the most beautiful structures in the landscape, and boy, do they provide privacy.

A walled front garden is a classic feature of Spanish architecture, both on the Mediterranean and in South America. We can still see this style in historic buildings in Louisiana, Florida, and the Southwest. I was struck by the mysterious beauty of these structures while walking down a residential street in an old section of New Orleans, on my way to visit my friends Mickey and George. Instead of front lawns, I passed a series of walls, green with ivy and moss. One entered the front yards through doorways made of stout wood or the curvaceous iron grillwork for which New Orleans is famous. Here and there through the openings, I could catch a glimpse of courtyard gardens beyond.

Leaving the dusty busy street and entering into such a courtyard was like coming into a soothing space away from the world, especially when I saw the small fountain trickling cool water in the midday heat and Mickey standing next to it with a tray of drinks. The entire courtyard was paved with aging brick. Herbs, tropical flowers, palms, and cyads were grown in pots clustered around the fountain and the front door. Shaded by thick wooden beams, well hung with bougainvillea vines, it seemed like *paradiso in terra* as we sat listening to Cajun music, nibbling Cajun chips, and guzzling Cajun beer in the sultry Louisiana afternoon. Son of a gun, we had some fun on the bayou.

Obviously, this courtyard arrangement was perfected in the days before air-conditioning. In the past, the only way to bring coolness to a hot climate was to shade the house from the southern and western sun and keep cool stone and precious water as close as possible.

The enclosed front courtyard design is more than old—it's positively ancient. You may have seen Cecil B. De Mille movies where biblical characters are having their feet washed in the well in the front courtyard by beautiful maidens wearing scarves. Those courtyards were the hearts of private houses in ancient times. But just because it's an old idea doesn't mean it isn't a fabulous one even today. It's a much more suitable garden for hot places like Phoenix and Orlando than the postage-stamp lawn surrounding the tract house trying to be yet another imitation Chatsworth on the Chattahoochee.

Even in twenty-first-century America, a stucco wall topped by rough-hewn beams would be a sensational place for growing bougainvillea, and the shade it provides will save on air-conditioning costs.

Fences

For complete privacy, the next best to an enduring stone or brick wall is a tall wooden fence. Formal tall wooden fences made of latticework or cutwork carpentry are beautiful—and expensive. Informal ones are cheaper. The choice depends upon the size of the property and the bank account of the owner.

I see plenty of inexpensive wooden fences around the countryside, mostly of a type called "stockade" by the lumberyards and home centers where they are sold. They are usually made of rustic unfinished pine, sometimes with the bark still intact on the outside. You may have noticed that such fences often really do live up to their name. They are supposed to evoke a sort of early American frontier look, and they do. They look about as friendly and inviting as the stockade around Fort Apache—from the point of view of Cochise! Aesthetically, they fit into the landscape about as well.

A stockade fence doesn't have to look bellicose, however. The way to make a stockade or board fence fit into the landscape more gracefully is to place it four to ten feet inside the edge of the property line, then plant the area between the fence and the property line with shrubs and trees. Ideally, the shrubs and trees you pick will be self-sustaining and easy to grow without a lot of watering and fertilizing. You don't want to spend the summer tending the area *outside* the garden wall. You want to plant it and forget it, except for a couple of times a year when you go in to chop weeds or to prune overgrowth. A few evergreens mixed in with flowering shrubs will help soften the fence all year-round. (More about using shrubs in the landscape later.)

Another way to make a wood fence more compatible with the landscape is either to stain it very dark brown or let it go gray and weathered-looking. Tip: You can give wood that gray, weathered patina instantly, using a simple home recipe. Plop a steel wool pad (the kind without soap) into a gallon of water, add a cup of vinegar, and let it stand overnight. Slop it on the fence with a roller the next day.

Of course, the best way to avoid an ugly fence is to erect a pretty one. An attractive fence will increase the value of the property many times more than the expense of putting one up. And the surefire way to make a fence look good is to make it compatible with the architecture of the house. In other words, the fence should be an extension of the house. For example, a ranch house with a board, split-rail, or simple picket fence is fine, because those are the kinds of fences that a real, authentic western buckaroo with a fifty-mile spread would have used around his genuine ranch house.

A fence around a split-level could have modern unadorned vertical lines made of nicely cut boards or treillage.

A colonial house cries out for elaborately fashioned white pickets, like the ones you see in Colonial Williamsburg.

More than any other style, the picket fence is traditionally American. (It has the same name as a Civil War hero, General Pickett, who led the famous charge at Gettysburg. And the Civil War was so American. *Both sides* were American. You can't get more American than that.) Originally, picket fences were employed to keep wandering livestock, grazing horses, or children from accidentally trampling or eating the front garden, and were in general use in city and farm until that front-lawn-as-public-park craze took over and the automobile made grazing horses obsolete.

While a four-foot picket fence does not provide complete privacy from the street the way a tall stone wall does (another Civil War general, by chance), it does define the space visually by putting a line around the front garden, the way a frame defines the edges of a picture. Psychologically, a four-foot fence clearly delineates personal space and acts as therapy for the American lack-of-boundary neurosis mentioned above.

You don't really have to slavishly follow the house architecture to make a nice fence. So few houses have distinctive architecture anyway that (in practice) any style of fence is suitable, as long as it is *less* formal than the house.

For example, a western-style split-rail fence around a house of indeterminate architecture, like a semi-colonial split-level, is appropriate. It is simple and less formal than the house. It doesn't fight the "architectural style," such as it is, but defines the boundary of the yard without calling too much attention to itself.

A fence that is more formal than the house can look laughable. Not far from where I live, a guy has put up an elaborate wrought-iron gate with a large bronze Maltese Cross on the top. It opens onto a short driveway that leads to a small two-bedroom modular ranch house with vinyl siding. Who does this guy think he is, I wonder, the Duke of Earl? Such a fancy gate in front of such a modest house makes me suspect that the guy is trying to make the ignorant think he is richer than he is, which is tacky, or he got the gate on sale when a cemetery went out of business and must have said to himself, "What the heck, at these prices, I *am* the Duke of Earl!" Do cemeteries go out of business? Maybe he stole it. I wouldn't be surprised with lousy taste like that.

The point is, don't overdo it. A fence is an accessory, like a necklace, a leather belt, or a tiara. It looks best when it goes with the outfit.

Wattle Fences

A wattle fence is an informal style that you rarely see in this country outside of garden magazines. It is a rustic fence that resembles a long basket. Properly woven, it will keep out most small pests like rodents, pets, and children. For a small cottage garden, a wattle fence is perfect.

A wattle fence has such Old World charm and simple elegance, it's practically medieval. It *is* medieval. We see it in woodcuts of monastery and castle gardens, and it probably dates back to Roman times or even earlier.

A wattle fence is so charming it brings tears to your eyes. If the uprights are made of cedar or pressure-treated wood, they will last for many years. All you have to do is add more woven branches every so often as the old ones get funky. Remember, this is a peasant folk-art fence, so it doesn't have to be perfect. In fact, it's better if it's not perfect. (Sure, much better, I tell myself.)

I made wattle fences in Madison Square Park in Manhattan to keep the dogs out of the flower beds. This was for the cable television show *Garden Variety*, which had a tight budget.

Since we were doing this in the middle of New York City, there wasn't too much green plant material to be had for the taking. The show had to buy grapevines from a florists' supply house. They cost a dollar a foot! That hurt! I must say the rustic fence enclosing a plot of flowers looked fabulous in contrast to the cityscape around it.

There is an easier way to make a wattle fence, which I discovered in Great Britain.

The first time I went to England, in early spring before the deciduous leaves emerged, I saw miles of woven fences along the narrow road. I was impressed! How do they have the patience to cut all those vines and weave them into fences, I asked myself, and how did they find the time? I was sure those thrifty *Anglaises* hadn't paid a dollar a foot for it.

Then I looked more closely. Those vines were alive! They had been planted at intervals and the ends had been woven in and out of uprights as the plant grew. When I came back to England in the summer, the wattle fences were not noticeable because they had leafed out and looked like hedgerows. What a great idea! It is much easier to weave a vine in and out of uprights as it grows than to gather long pieces of grapevine and lug them around the countryside. Of course, if you sold them in New York City, they'd be worth more than a block of tickets to *Cats*.

Wattle structures aren't only for people with unlimited time and/or independent incomes. You'd be amazed at what can be done with only a little talent and imagination.

One of the loveliest wattle structures I have ever seen was at the Philadelphia Flower Show last year. It was part of the Philadelphia Green exhibit. Philadelphia Green is an organization that turns empty, junk-filled, urban lots into community gardens. This wattle structure was not a fence, but an eight-foot-high arbor made of grapevines loosely woven across four rusticated uprights that looked like tree trunks. It was large enough to put seats underneath the shady tangle of graceful, twisted vines. The shape was decidedly imperfect, and so uneven that one side almost obscured the opening, making the area underneath a secret place, inviting the most intimate conversation,

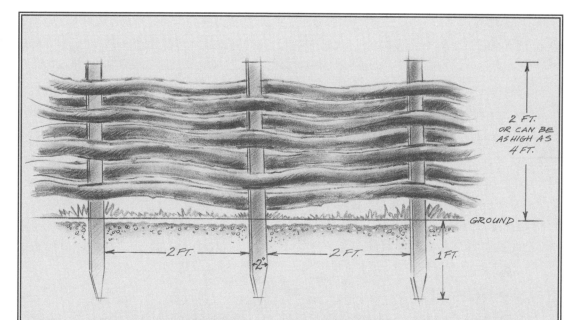

To make a wattle fence, you need to space upright posts at two-foot intervals. The posts should be at least two inches thick and sunk one foot into the ground. Whether you make a low two-foot rabbit fence or decide to go for the four-foot height, the posts need to be sturdy, because they will be the warp around which you will weave the fence.

The best material for weaving is new wood that can bend without breaking. Very slender branches of green wood about a half-inch (½") to an inch and a half (1½") in diameter are excellent. In the old days, willow was grown especially for this purpose. I use wild grape, although other woody vines or long flexible green branches will do just as well. Wild grape is a rampant weed in my area that especially favors waste places of new growth woods or the shoulder of the highway where weed trees have begun to spring up, so it's plentiful.

To start the wattle fence, gather all the material you can. (For easy transport, I gather the long vines or branches into large circles the way a cowboy carries rope.) To start the fence, weave the flexible branches in and out between the uprights, as though you were making the world's largest basket. It helps if you don't have a steady job, because making a wattle fence is time-consuming. Weave it as tightly as you can, under one post and over the next. You don't have to weave every other row differently. Two or more branches can be woven in and out together. This makes a larger pattern.

spiritual contemplation, or hot make-out session. The crowd at the flower show oohed and ahhed over it.

To find out how it was made, I called Sally McCabe. She and Janet Carter of Philadelphia Green knew all about it because it was their exhibit. Sally and Janet are gardeners after my own heart. They take gardening seriously, but they aren't solemn about it.

"Well, we had these weedy locust tree saplings in the empty lot we were making into a garden," Sally explained to me on the phone. "There were tons of grapevines on the site, so we kind of wove them in and out of the branches of the saplings to make the arbor. Basically, we started them at the base and worked them over the tops all day until we ran out of vines. Then it was done."

"The trees were alive?" I asked, somewhat shocked by her cavalier attitude, which I liked.

"I presume so, although in February, when we put the thing together, there were no leaves on the trees or the grapevines, so who knows?"

"So the trees will sprout leaves?"

"Not anymore. We chopped them down to bring the arbor to the flower show," she said with the sangfroid of a medical examiner doing an autopsy. "They're dead, but there are plenty of others in the lot. We'll make another arbor and prune out any branches that look wrong," she informed me without a touch of remorse. "Then we'll let the trees leaf out and even bloom if they are so inclined. Locusts have nice flowers. Is that what you wanted to know?"

"Yeah, thanks."

At that point the conversation turned to merits of the other exhibits and gossip about other gardeners, subjects that are outside the parameters of this book.

The point is that you can make an award-winning, artistic structure using only the materials at hand.

Hedges

The other classic enclosure for a front yard is a hedge. A hedge is a row of shrubs usually, but not necessarily, clipped to form what can only be described as a topiary wall. I love tall hedges, but even four-foot hedges are neat and nostalgic, and define spaces very well. A neighbor of mine planted a couple of bundles of privet about four years ago and now they are eight feet tall and provide a green, reasonably friendly, non-threatening boundary between his house and the street. (It's no coincidence that the word *privet* has the same root as the word *private*.) He added a wooden arch to mark the entrance where the front walk meets the street. That hedge provides almost complete privacy from cars and pedestrians, and I would bet he and his wife do it more than the national average.

In my zone-five climate, privet is not evergreen, as it would be in warmer parts of the country, but even without the leaves, it acts like a wall. That eight-foot hedge is about two feet thick and so dense that you'd have to be a dedicated Peeping Tom to see anything through it. In fact, you have to stick your head into the hedge and practically poke your eye out to see anything, and you can get quite a nasty scratch across the nose doing that, believe me. It took several weeks to heal.

The way to make a good-looking hedge instead of a scraggly one is to keep the top slightly narrower than the bottom, thereby allowing light to reach the lower branches. You often see hedges with wide tops and a mess of twiggy bare branches at the bottom. That's because the top shades out the lower branches, causing them to lose their leaves.

The guy who cuts the hedges in front of the old folks' home across the street from my house does them that way and it drives me crazy. Whenever I see him, I want to run over and tell him the right way to do it, but his red-plaid hunter's cap and gas-powered hedge trimmer look threatening, and I shrink from giving unsolicited gardening advice to a man I suspect has an AK-47 rifle under the front seat of his Dodge pickup. If he ever asked me, I would tell him that a hedge should be shaped like a wedge with the widest part at the bottom. "Remember the motto: A hedge is a wedge!" I would advise cheerily as I backed away slowly.

Evergreen hedges are terrific, although deer love yew. I love yew, too. Hemlock will do well in sun or shade. Arborvitae is beautiful. Cedar is poetic. Pines and spruces can't be sheared like yew or hemlock, but they are stately in large landscapes, where their eventual size is a plus. (But they are a nightmare in small yards, where their eventual size is like having a brontosaurus nesting in the front yard.)

Many people think that the only good hedge is evergreen and clipped, but you can make a hedge out of any kind of shrub that grows thickly enough to provide enclosure.

While deciduous shrubs don't provide as much privacy in the winter because the leaves are gone, they do fine in the spring, summer, and fall, and that's when you use the garden the most anyway. Many deciduous shrubs have beautiful flowers, interesting leaves, or colorful berries. Deutzia (*Deutzia rosea*) has pale blossoms in late spring and grows to about six feet; upright cotoneaster (*Cotoneaster Simonsii*) grows to six feet and has beautiful berries through the winter; northern bayberry (*Myrica pensylvanica*) is a native American with white berries that takes well to shearing. Another wonder shrub is the upright firethorn (*Pyracantha coccinea*), heavily laden with bright orange-red berries, densely branched, and easily trimmed to any height. And I won't even mention shrub roses and the other excellent candidates, which are available in catalogs, nurseries, and plant sales everywhere. All that stands between you and a beautiful hedge is time and money, not necessarily in that order.

Flowering hedges are considered informal and as such they don't need to be clipped. In fact, most flowering shrubs look best when allowed to grow into their own natural shape and look pathetic when sheared into boxes and gumdrops.

There's a rectangular lilac bush in front of the old folks' home. Needless to say, it is the creation of the mean-looking man in the hunter's cap, the same guy who mangles the hedges.

Last week, I passed him while he was shearing the top off the lilac. I must have stumbled or something, because he stopped and turned to glare at me, the hedge trimmer still vibrating noisily in his paw. "How do you like it?" He leered insanely, indicating the bush with his weapon.

"Nice lilac," I stammered insincerely.

"It's a refrigerator." He seemed proud of himself.

The way to get a deciduous hedge for free is to ask a neighbor to let you take divisions from his shrubs. You can take ten or twenty sucker-like shoots with their roots attached before he will notice and start to feel like a sucker himself. Thank him profusely and suggest that you'd love to have him and the wife over to dinner sometime, but don't give a specific date. Perhaps in the winter, you might suggest, when there's not so much work to do in the yard.

Then take the divisions home and plant them in a row, six feet apart—more or less according to the eventual size of the shrub. Baby these little branches for the first year by watering them at least once a week, if not more. It is absolutely imperative that they don't dry out, especially in the fall and winter of those first twelve months. In about three to five years the little suckers will grow into an informal hedge whose height will depend on the type of shrub you have selected. I know three to five years is a long time when you're middle-aged and older. But what do you want? You've just glommed several hundred dollars' worth of shrubs for free, for heaven's sake. In three to five years your neighbor will have forgotten about that dinner, also.

"Ah, a topiary refrigerator! Of course! Why didn't I see it before? Fabulous. Did you know that a hedge is a wedge?" I ventured.

"What?"

"A hedge is a wedge."

He turned off the hedge shears. "Hey, lady, are you trying to tell me that if I made the top of this hedge slightly narrower than the bottom, it would solve the problem of those unsightly bare branches at the base?"

"Yes."

"Thank you, thank you, Miss, Ms. . . . I don't even know your name."

"Greenthumbs. *Mrs.* Greenthumbs," I said with quiet modesty. "Ever heard of me?"

"No."

"Oh."

"Well, so long, Mrs. Greenbuns, and thank you."

Of course that conversation never really happened, but many flowering shrubs, such as hydrangeas, camellias, and smoke bushes have rounded shapes, while others such as spireas, weigelas, forsythias, and brooms look more like fountains. A long row of fountain-shaped shrubs is as lovely as a waterfall. Okay, it won't sound like a waterfall, but it looks really nice, especially when in bloom.

The Shrub Border

Less formal than a hedge of one variety of flowering shrub is a combination of different shrubs planted in a row at the edge of your property line. But there is a right way and a wrong way to do this. In fact, my father did it the wrong way on Long Island. After a few years, the different shrubs began to grow together. Instead of forming a continuous shape with uniform height and width, they grew at different rates and began to shade each other out. At this point my father clipped them all back to the bone to keep them separated for their own good. Now he no longer had a hedge that would have made an enclosure for his garden (what garden?), but a collection of small shrubs five feet apart that looked like bric-a-brac lined up on the mantelpiece (what mantelpiece?).

The right way to make a fantastic wall out of a variety of shrubs is by staggering them, putting the taller ones in the back and the shorter ones in front as you would in a flower border. When they grow into each other, let them. Cut back only if it is a life or death situation for you or the shrubs. As the shrubs come in and out of bloom, the collection will enclose the garden with a thick border of flowering, dense growth, which is the whole point of this chapter.

When planning a flowering shrub border, it's a good design principle to repeat the same variety three times. Repetition makes a pattern. The other shrubs will seem as though they were deliberately chosen to accompany the star plant, instead of a motley crew of odds and ends that you may have bought on sale in the nursery in August.

In England, they have something called a tapestry hedge. It's a hedge made of several different kinds of shrubs grown closely together and sheared to a uniform height and width. It's a nice idea, but you have to prune it religiously or it looks messy, since the faster growing plants tend to stick out of the slower growing ones. When it's kept properly clipped, it's very beautiful, especially in the fall when the leaves turn different colors and it really does look like a tapestry.

The truth is, many plants can be made into hedges. For example, a very effective and unique fencing material is the old-fashioned cactus hedge, used in Texas and the West.

Other Solutions

Whatever the style, whether you have a tall stone or brick wall for maximum enclosure, or a four-foot hedge or a picket fence to define psychological boundaries, the straight lines of a fence organize the space and make sense of it. Straight lines give the impression, however erroneous, that everything in this home is under control. Most important, the straight lines of a fence give visual proportion and a point of reference to the plantings.

See for yourself. Go out into a weedy lot. It's just a mess of weeds, right? Now place two vertical posts anywhere in the lot and walk around them. Suddenly the weeds create a pattern that wasn't there before! Look, a drift of goldenrod lies between the posts, a patch of daisies seems to be designed to go in front of them. There was no "front" before! Those posts have defined a space and provided a point of reference. The place now seems more like a garden or a room, the beginning of order out of chaos—civilization!

Now take those same upright posts and place them at the outer corners of your front yard. Amazing, isn't it? You have just defined the boundary to your property with the universal phallic symbols of domain, two eight-foot wooden poles. The structures are full of meaning, and they look pretty good, too. You could stop right there and plant some roses to climb up those posts and have a couple of nice symmetrical garden ornaments, or you could go ahead and plant more posts, run metal chains between them, and train husky plants like wisteria or red trumpet vine to grow along the chains to make a living garland. Or you could go ahead and put fencing between the posts with a beautiful gate in the middle. I swear that anything you plant along that fence will look great.

Look at gardens in magazines. Almost every photo has a structure, often a wall or fence, along with the flowers. It works in the photos. Take the hint.

PLEASE NOTE: Traditional colors to use when painting a fence are white, dark green, brown, or black, but for a small yard, it looks interesting to use the same color as the house trim.

ANOTHER NOTE: You should erect a metal chain-link fence in the front yard only if you own a pit bull. And please place the mailbox outside the gate—your postal service will thank you.

GARDEN ROOMS

What I Learned in England

Front yards become more interesting if you use fences and hedges, but garden structures do a lot for the rest of the yard as well. Fences, hedges, and arbors can be used to separate the yard into sections, each with its own purpose, design, and theme. In

England, these sections are known as "garden rooms." I got to see quite a few of them last summer as the result of a miracle.

It all started when a man named Tom Baugh asked me if I would appear at his home-and-garden show in Akron, Ohio. Naturally, I accepted. I've always wanted to see Akron in February.

An Englishman named Michael Franks, the producer of a live home-and-garden show in London called the *Ideal Home Exhibition,* happened to be in Akron that weekend on a tour of American shows, looking for speakers and he hired me on the spot.

Two weeks later, my husband, Walter, and I were in London! As soon as our plane landed, we were whisked off to romantic Liverpool, where I was to do a promotional gardening segment on a British morning talk show called *This Morning with Richard and Judy.*

The hosts interview celebrities and do segments on cooking, gardening, fashion, etc. Richard and Judy are married to each other but don't get along too well, which gives the show plenty of built-in tension. For my segment, I wanted to demonstrate that you can use almost anything as a planter. I planted petunias in an old coffeepot, ivy in a pair of sneakers, a rosemary in a handbag, that sort of thing.

The show is live, so you have to carry on, no matter what. And of course everything went wrong. The plants fell apart, Richard made fun of my accent, which annoyed Judy, the rosemary wouldn't fit into the handbag, etc. To make a long story short, they liked it. In fact, they asked me back to do a series of garden segments for them. The producer, Melanie, a camera crew, and director would videotape me as I visited ten famous English gardeners over the course of two weeks that summer, and then the interviews would be shown on the program the following spring. Do you understand what I'm saying? Granada Television was going to *pay* me to tour English gardens! I was hired to look at gardens. In England. See what I mean by a miracle?

To sweeten the deal, they even paid for Walter to come with me, which meant that I would be working, but Walter would have nothing to do but be my boy-toy. It was an unusual role for a gray-haired, middle-aged manager of a New York commuter railroad, but he got used to it very quickly. I had to talk him out of getting his navel pierced.

It was really quite an honor to represent America on British TV because the English have a reputation for being incredibly snobbish about American gardeners. Most of the gardening literature comes from them to us, rather than vice versa.

One of the loveliest gardens on the tour belonged to Lady Mary Keen. When I heard the title before I met her, in a fit of reverse snobbery I thought, "Aristocratic. *Her* ancestors never landed on Ellis Island." After I met her, it took me a good two seconds to get over it, and then two more to fall in love with her. Not that way. She is a talented, earthy gardener who has my highest respect.

Mary is a tall, robust woman with a young rosy face framed by soft almost-white hair, and you can tell she gets along with nature very well. Not only is she an extraordinary gardener, but she has a wonderful sense of humor, a strapping husband, and handsome grown children.

She made an impromptu lunch for us in her dream kitchen. *My* dream kitchen. I don't mean it had Formica countertops and fancy appliances everywhere, like the kitchen behind door number two on *The Price Is Right*. No, we sat at a long wooden farmhouse table that was covered by a blue-and-white-checkered cotton tablecloth. Against the creamy yellow walls were open-shelved cabinets, which held dishes that looked like old or handmade pottery—not just for show—the same dishes we were using. I was too polite to turn over the plate to see what kind of china it was, since Mary was in the room at all times.

Mary Keen's lunch was good, but her garden was extraordinary. It consisted of a series of garden rooms, marked off by hedges or stone walls, which are common in England.

The great thing I learned from Mary Keen was that each garden room should have an idea, a feeling all its own—in other words, a theme.

How to Create a Theme for Each Garden Room

Mary Keen told me about the thought process she goes through in deciding what to put in a garden: "It helps to sum up what I am trying to do in a mantra of adjectives, which describes the desired effect. 'Ancient, peaceful, timeless, green, humble'—these are the words that made a useful formula for the kitchen garden below the tower of the Saxon church."* (Okay, so she has a view of a thousand-year-old Saxon church in her yard. So you don't. Stop sniveling. Neither do I. If you have a lousy view, plant a hedge in front of it and create mystery.)

Anyway, everything she did in that garden illustrated those words, the structures she used were rusticated wood and "humble," the plantings were of "peaceful" fruit trees, berries, and vegetables. The word *green* suggested the paths, which were of grass instead of asphalt or gravel. Only the center of the path was mown short for walking. The rest was allowed to grow long and "timeless." The "ancient" part was the church itself and the hills beyond the garden walls. Keeping her descriptive words constantly in mind gave the area a focus and a simplicity of purpose, so she always knew what to put in and what to leave out.

Okay, we may not all be real artists and garden poets like Mary, but anyone can come up with a few defining ideas that will make decisions easier and give the garden a point of view that makes it all "click," so to speak. You know what I mean. That "look" that "works." That artistic "something" that makes us "admire" and secretly "resent" those who have "it."

She also says you should stick to one theme for roughly every sixty-five to seventy square feet. That is six-by-ten feet or seven-by-nine feet—think of it as the size of the average flower bed. It doesn't mean that you can't make the area larger than that. In fact you should if you can, but don't make it smaller or you will have a hodgepodge of conflicting ideas, which will look like no theme at all.

In practice, Mary kept one theme for each garden room. She had an area that adjoined a very sunny, brightly colored garden. This area was about fifty by fifty feet and sloped downward. Instead of trying to level it off, she made stairs that descended into the space and then enclosed it with a hedge. She used plants with white and pale-

*Mary Keen, *Creating a Garden* (London: Conran Octopus, 1996). Actually, I am quoting Mary Keen's book, but she said the same thing to me in person. I only mention the book to give her point more weight and her book a nice plug. She didn't ask me to do it.

colored flowers. Coming from the bright garden, the descent into this pale dell seemed to me like quiet after noise, peace after riot, sadness after gaiety. Mary was delighted that I understood her meaning. Her theme words for this garden were "sad, pale, mournful, peaceful."

Mary Keen also recommends that you use other gardens for inspiration. In other words, steal from the great ones, which is what I'm doing right now.

How to Lay Out Garden Rooms

Not only does Mary Keen's vegetable garden look out over a medieval stone church, it covers a large area and is located amid gently sloping hills. Not all of us are lucky enough to have a yard in the romantic English countryside with lots of interesting landscapes. In fact, most of our backyards have no view at all. They are flat spaces of mostly grass that the viewer takes in at one glance and have all the visual mystery of a high school gymnasium. The way to add magic, romance, and a sense of place is to do what Mary Keen did in her romantic situation: subdivide a gym-size area into three or four garden rooms, each with a clear theme, simple design, or at least a definite purpose.

Houses in crowded suburbs have yards that are a lot smaller than gymnasiums. But stay with me, because whether you have space for one, two, or three garden rooms, these suggestions will produce the most beautiful garden you can imagine.

For practical reasons, the garden rooms should require less maintenance as you go farther away from the house. The room nearest the house, the one you see most often, will inevitably get the most attention, but unless you are a person who likes to hide away from it all, the area at the back of a large yard will be ignored much of the time.

Garden rooms do not have to follow each other in a row like cars on a subway train. Depending on the shape of the yard, the lay of the land, and your own preference, there are many possibilities. Here are just a few:

1. A large central room with smaller grottos and gardens around it, like private rooms around the main dining room of a restaurant.

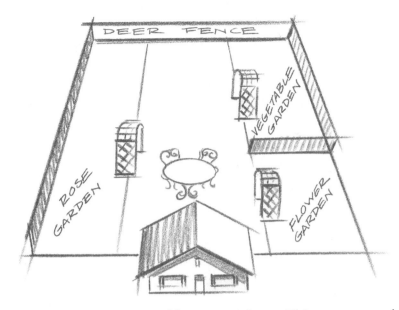

2. Two large garden rooms separated by a grove of trees. This arrangement has a lot of drama, since it means you go from a sunny open area into a mysterious one and then out into sunshine again. It is very satisfying psychologically. If you've ever had a bad night and then felt your spirits lifted in the morning sunshine, you know how good that feels.

3. Garden rooms connected by an allée of trees or a long wisteria-covered series of arches that lead the visitor from one garden to the next, as bedrooms lead off a hallway.

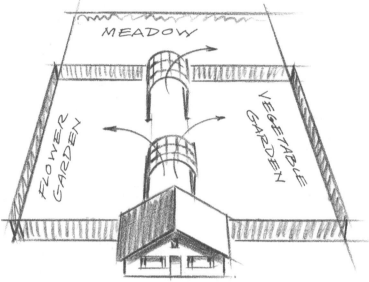

4. A series of wide passageways at right angles to one another. One of the best garden layouts I've ever seen reminded me of Wal-Mart, and I mean that as a compliment. It was set up as a series of long aisles flanked by trees, shrubs, or flower borders.

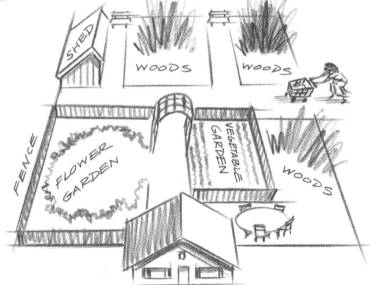

Think of the way a discount department store is arranged, with long aisles flanked by plastic housewares, knockoff perfumes, canned goods, gallon drums of potato chips, hunting equipment, etc. The aisles intersect at right angles and are wide enough for four people to pass one another. Whenever you turn a corner, there is a change of theme. This injects an element of surprise, even anticipation into the walk around the store. Here's bulk candy, but turn the corner—what will it be?—plastic dishpans! What's beyond that—holy moly!— it's men's underwear! The arrangement is not accidental. These stores were structured to be as inviting as possible, based on years of consumer research.

Now imagine that instead of an acre occupied by a warehouse filled with junky stuff, this is an acre of land. Between rows of shrubs or evergreens, aisles are wide swathes of grass or gravel, flanked by roses. The tall shrubs or evergreen hedges obscure the view beyond them. Another aisle runs at right angles to the first one, turn the corner and—what is it?—vegetables in rows. The peas and tomatoes growing on rustic fences that form the aisles. Just beyond, it all opens up into a grassy space with a small pool or picnic table in the center.

These garden layouts assume that you have started making your garden on a bare piece of land with nothing growing on it. In fact, now that suburbia is more than a few generations old, it's pretty hard to find an absolutely "unimproved" tract. Older suburban homes often have mature shrubs or trees scattered in inconvenient places around the property.

What to Do About Badly Placed Shrubs

Unless you have bought a new house on an empty tract, you have probably inherited some shrubs. Undoubtedly, there are some foundation plantings in front of the house, and often there are a few other bushes plunked here and there in the corner of the front lawn or the middle of the backyard. The first thing most people want to do is bulldoze the whole thing and start all over again. Wait! Don't pull anything out unless you absolutely have to! Large shrubs give weight, substance, and sense of place to a garden, and they constitute valuable plant material for the new garden design. If the specimen is the type of shrub that grows by sending sucker-like shoots up next to itself, dig some of the shoots with a bit of root attached and plant more of that fellow. Use him as the starting point for the shrub border or shrub hedge I described earlier.

Is a plant a him or a her? Ships are referred to as she, but that is just naval tradition. I like to think of plants as either he or she depending on their appearance, but these are my own arbitrary nicknames. In fact, with a few exceptions, most bushes are both he and she in one. There are male plants named Holly, however. I hesitate to draw any social metaphor from this.

Is Mother Nature on the side of bisexuality, or is each plant a monogamous married couple? It depends on your point of view. And where is Father Nature in all this? Is Mother Nature a single mom? Who supports her and all of us children? God? I remember as a child I had the idea that God was the poppa and Mother Nature was the momma. Later I discovered that this idea was heresy, or at least nonsense in most major world religions, and I could go to hell for it in a dozen languages. Nowadays, I stick to gardening.

Some people hate forsythias, spireas, or mock oranges, just because they are so familiar, but many of the old shrubs you find around an old house are the common varieties because they are the ones that have survived from one house owner to the next. If you want trendy shrubs, go ahead and plant them in addition to those old troopers that have proven their toughness and durability. Don't dig up Grandma's quince just because the blooms are a revolting lipstick coral pink that clash with the golden daffodils! Just because she wasn't *your* grandma! Use your imagination. Cut the yellow daffodils and bring them into the house as soon as they bloom, then dig them up. Flank that quince with two or three flowering almonds, which have pale peachy-colored blossoms and bloom at about the same time. Now the picture is a symphony of warm pink and coral, and the quince looks more ravishing than revolting. Around the shrubs, plant some pink, blue, and white hyacinths, blue *Chionodoxa,* royal blue *Scilla sibirica,* and white daffodils with apricot pink cups that echo the coral of the quince. Now you have a spring garden that's to die for.

Try to work awkwardly placed shrubs into the garden design. A shrub rose plunked in the middle of the back lawn is ungainly most of the year and pathetic when it blooms alone in June. Look upon this unfortunate placement as an opportunity. Use the shrub rose as a dividing line between garden rooms. Place an arch next to the rosebush, then plant a climbing rose variety of the same color on the other side of the arch. That arrangement will become the rear wall of the first room and the entrance to the second.

It's even better to have two shrubs in the middle of the yard. Place an arch between them and the two shrubs immediately become a wall with a doorway in it. Complete the wall by taking suckers of the existing shrubs and planting them in a row to form the back wall of a garden room, or (great fun) find other shrubs to bloom at different times in the same or contrasting colors and shapes and make a shrub border between garden rooms.

If there is an especially beautiful shrub or tree in the center of the yard, such as a flowering crab or magnolia, place the fence or hedge just behind it to frame this natural work of art.

Don't be afraid to place the opening to the next room over to one side of the area. As I tell myself when I look at my face in the mirror, symmetry isn't everything. There's no law that says the opening has to be in the center, or that there has to be only one entrance. A path that goes around an object and disappears into the trees invites exploration.

Despite all efforts to use it in the landscape, sometimes it's necessary to move a shrub. You have to do something about a bush that has been planted too close to the house or to a path when it was little, so that now it grabs your scarf or pokes you in the eye whenever you go by. The easiest way to move a large shrub is in stages.

HOW TO MOVE A SHRUB

1. *In spring,* dig a deep trench all around the shrub about two feet from the base, severing as many of its roots as you can. This will force the shrub to grow all its roots in a confined area all summer.

2. *The following fall,* dig the hole to receive the shrub. It should be twice as wide as the root ball, but it doesn't have to be twice as deep. Prune large branches of the shrub before moving it. Many garden books say to cut all the branches back by one third, but I only cut the biggest ones.

3. *The next day,* invite one or two strong friends for lunch, and when they ask you what they should bring for dessert, tell them "shovels." With a little help from your friends, finish digging under the shrub and lever it out of the hole and onto a sheet or blanket.

4. Drag it over to the new hole and plant it in good earth, keeping it at the same soil level as it was in the original hole. You don't have to stomp on the earth to pack it. Instead, stick your fingers into the fresh soil so that the water will be guided toward the roots to settle the soil and get rid of air pockets. Water deeply.

5. Mulch well and water once a week. Don't feed a newly transplanted shrub until the following year.

Garden Buildings

Many people buy little wooden or corrugated metal toolsheds to store garden supplies. Because they are so ugly, people tend to place them at the back of the garden, out of sight, but they are very useful as part of a garden wall between rooms. Covered in treillage, which you can buy at the lumberyard in eight-foot sheets (the lumberman might

call it lattice), a garden toolshed is a wonderful place to grow ivy, roses, espaliered fruit trees, sweet peas, Mexican gourds, etc. Place a bench in front of the shed, flanked by pots of herbs, and the whole thing will look like a magazine photo. Incidentally, this ready-made treillage is great for covering all kinds of ugly buildings, obscuring unsightly views, and generally dressing up the place.

The First Garden Room

We will call the area closest to the back of the house the first room. It's the one you will see most of the time, and it is the area you will pay the most attention to on a daily or weekend basis. Realistically, it may be the only area you have time to pay attention to, if you work all week. This room should be the one most heavily planted, either with flowers or vegetables.

If the area next to the house is a terrace or patio or deck, that's the place for ornamental plantings. If you don't entertain a lot and the area is adjacent to the kitchen at the back of the house, it's the perfect place for a kitchen garden.

If you have young children, a play area outside the kitchen window will keep them under a supervising eye and a fence will keep them from running out. This arrangement works just as well for puppies.

This first room doesn't have to be large. In fact, do yourself a favor and keep it small. Many gardens look sparse and bare because people are trying to make a few plants fill a large area. A half-acre space with few plants looks like a long buffet table

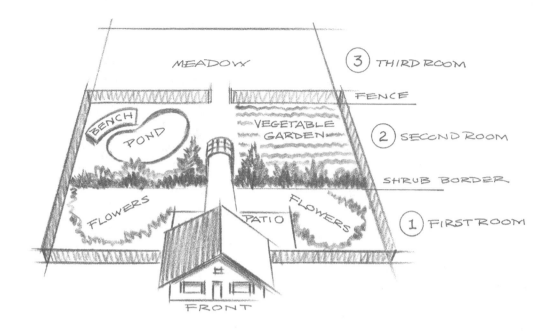

with four dishes on it, stingy and unsatisfying. But if you keep the planted area relatively small, it is easy to fill up—more like a coffee table with four dishes on it. You would be amazed at the number of plants that will grow in a twenty-by-twenty-foot space, especially if they are closely planted. Plants growing cheek by jowl look full and have that cottage garden *je ne sais quoi*. Their interlocking branches also shade out weeds.

How to Place Flower Borders

Most of the time you see a garden with a lawn in the center and flower borders around the edges. This is a pleasant arrangement, and there is nothing wrong with it. But you don't have to plant flowers around the perimeter of the garden room any more than you have to put all the furniture against the walls of the living room. One of the best ways to set up a flower border is to use the "bowling alley" model.

Imagine you are standing at the end of the alley with your fingers in a ball, looking at the pins. That is the way you should design flower borders, as seen from your most frequent viewing place. This means placing flower borders in rows leading away from where you're standing. That way, it's much harder to see spaces between the plants, emerging weeds, or anything that is out of bloom. You may have noticed that flowers at the peak of their bloom stand out and those that are spent tend to fall over. With a border that moves away from the eye, all you see are the plants that are in full bloom. Gardens in magazines are often photographed with the camera at one end looking down the spine of the border, because they look best that way.

Hugh Johnson, the wine expert, was one of the famous English gardeners I met on my miracle tour. In his garden, he had a large statue of a heavyset Victorian woman clutching her breast—a dominating figure, to say the least. I called her LaVerne Valera, after a friend of mine who makes dramatic gestures like that. Most people would have put flower borders horizontally to the left and right of LaVerne, like a frame. Instead, Hugh Johnson arranged the borders so that they led the eye up to the statue, then continued behind her. Sections of the border were separated by brick paths, and the statue was placed in the central intersection, as though she were standing between bowling lanes. At the end farthest from my vantage point, two tall, upright junipers marked the end of the view.

THE ONLY SUREFIRE WAY TO KEEP DEER, WOODCHUCKS, GOPHERS, AND RABBITS OUT OF THE GARDEN ROOM

I've tried every kind of repellent in my garden: bad-tasting sprays, soap suspended from nylon stockings hanging off the trees (attractive to clean-foot fetishists), dried blood, camphor balls, human hair provided by a local beauty parlor, human pee distributed by Walter, even buckshot or arrows provided by my bow-hunting neighbor John. I have found these remedies bothersome and ineffective. The only surefire way to keep these creatures out and still have a normal life is to put up a fence, period. In an open area, where deer can get a running start, an eight- or even ten-foot fence is necessary. This can be an eight-foot fence with two feet of handsome barbed wire strung across the top.

A solid, six-foot fence should be high enough if you have shrubs planted on either side of it, since deer don't like to jump into brambles. A solid, opaque fence is better than a chain, wire, or rail fence, since deer can't see through it and don't like to jump into places they can't see. Would you?

An alternative to a very high fence is to place two four-foot fences parallel to each other and about four and a half feet apart. Deer are great high jumpers, but are not good at the broad jump. A four-foot snow fence with another four-foot snow fence behind it will be too much for the rascals. Ha, ha.

To keep large burrowing rodents, such as woodchucks, rabbits, and gophers, out of the garden, attach chicken wire along the bottom of the fence and bury it at least a foot and a half deep. If you can't dig that deeply, either because of rocks, impossible soil, or lack of ambition, the chicken wire will work almost as well if you attach one side to the bottom of the fence and lay the rest on top of the soil on the outside of the fence. When the bunny or gopher tries to dig under, he will be standing on the chicken wire. Ha, ha.

I designed my borders as seen from my side porch in just this way. Viewed from the house, longways, they look good even without LaVerne (I have a birdbath). When in doubt, think of the bowling alley and make that spare!

We who live in parts of the country infested with deer, woodchucks, and gophers have to keep the first room a manageable size because, if we want to garden at all, it has to be small enough to fence completely for a reasonable amount of money. In my experience, there is only one surefire way to keep mammal pests, such as deer, woodchucks, gophers, and rabbits out of my garden (see previous page).

The Second Room

If you have enclosed your entire yard, then a low fence or hedge, or even a shrub border with an arch in the middle, can act as a doorway to the second garden.

Even if you forgo the hedge, fence, or shrubs, either because they are too expensive or because you have a view of the Rocky Mountains you don't want to obscure, a line of vertical uprights, such as white marble Ionic columns, will separate the two areas

WOODS

FENCE
WITH
ARCH

SHRUB
BORDER

PATH   LAWN

visually and psychologically. Wooden porch posts or rustic wooden posts will do if white marble Ionic columns are unavailable, for some reason.

What you do with the second room will depend upon what happens in the first one. If the area closest to the house has the theme "flowers, abundance, color," then this is the place for "games, recreation, green." It may contain a croquet lawn, putting green, a set of garden swings, swimming pool, or picnic table. If the first garden contains flowers, the second garden might have a vegetable plot, a small orchard, or a low maintenance area, such as a pond or a meadow. If you have used the first room as a child's play area, then the second room is where to put the flower garden. Whatever it contains, the second room should have a table and chairs or at least a bench. *Every garden room should have a place to sit.* Without a place to sit, it's not a room, it's a vestibule.

What to Sit On

Fortunately, you don't need much furniture outdoors. Often a plank of wood supported by a couple of big rocks is sufficient to qualify. But let's face it, it's not as comfy as a table and cushioned chairs under an overhanging roof or a big umbrella.

When I started my garden twelve years ago, stylish garden pieces, like Chippendale garden benches and Victorian wicker porch sets, were as expensive as they are now, but other types of garden furniture were not. Walter and I could still find metal chairs from the 1950s in the town dump for free. Adirondack chairs, with their slanted backs and wide armrests suitable for holding iced-tea glasses, were auctioned off at a dollar apiece when old Catskill hotels closed. My relatives sat on many a hotel porch on those chairs in the 1940s and 1950s—flirting, drinking, kibitzing, complaining. What tales those chairs could tell!

Since then, those Adirondack chairs have become so fashionable, I've seen them featured indoors in shelter magazines like *House Beautiful.* I wouldn't be surprised to see my mother's aluminum lawn chairs with plastic webbing showing up in the dining rooms of trendy Manhattan lofts some day soon.

Garden furniture is sold everywhere. Even some pretty good metal mesh designs are sold in mass outlets at reasonable prices. Wooden director's chairs with canvas seats and backs can't be left out all winter, but they are nice and cheap at furniture outlets. Plastic chairs are very cheap. I don't like plastic in the garden, but I have to admit that the dark green ones aren't so bad. Yes, there is no shortage of garden furniture. Too bad there are so few gardens to put it in!

My aunt Dotty complains that she doesn't like to sit outside because there are bugs out there.

"You're right, Aunt Dotty," I tell her. "Bugs have been outdoors for millions of years."

"I'm here now. Make them leave!"

"Here, douse yourself with this." I give her Skin So Soft, a moisturizer that insects find repulsive. I find Dotty repulsive, but apparently the insects are not so discriminating.

"That's not good enough!" she decided, after dabbing it on like cologne.

"Why don't you go inside?"

"It's too hot inside. Why don't you get air-conditioning?"

"It's almost fall; it will be cool soon."

"Then it will be winter and then it will be cold."

At that point *I* go inside, looking for a spider to place on the arm of that fashionable Adirondack chair.

What exactly did Miss Muffet sit on when that spider came by, anyway? What is a tuffet? Actually, a tuffet is an herb-covered garden seat. Historically, garden seats were built into the garden walls, either in niches or as extensions, with the wall as the seat back. Medieval gardeners planted grass, thyme, chamomile, or other soft springy material right on top of the stone as a fragrant cushion. Grass must have been damp after a rain, but thyme or chamomile growing on the stone bench would have dried out a lot more quickly than the foam rubber cushion on a modern *chaise longue*. (You notice I wrote *chaise longue* and not chaise lounge. *Longue* is French and means "long" chair, not "lounge" chair. You probably knew this, but I didn't until my editor told me.)

Speaking of *chaises longues,* those very comfortable poolside chair-beds don't have to be confined to the cabana. Now that sunbathing is considered hazardous to the health, a *chaise longue* under the trees is restful and healthful, and in a well-enclosed garden, extremely convenient for serious dating, if you catch my drift. A hammock is good, too, if you're young and double-jointed.

In general, the best site for placing garden furniture, such as tables and chairs, is near the source of the food. Usually, that's the kitchen door. A table and chairs set more than twenty feet from the kitchen won't be used like one that is right outside the door near the coffeepot.

Beyond its function as a place to sit, eat, drink, read, or make out, a garden seat is a destination. To get to a destination, you need a path.

Garden Paths

Meandering garden paths are romantic, but we all know even a hot romance should go somewhere. In a garden room the paths should lead in and out of entrances, navigate changes in levels, lead from a porch or patio to another part of the yard, and they should do so with directness and authority.

If you are not sure where to put a garden path, start at the house door, then walk over to the back of the garden room taking the shortest route possible. Put your path where you just walked. Add a bench facing back toward the path, and you have made not just a path but a destination, and most important, you have made a room. The bench is now a focal point around which to plant topiary animals, display pots of herbs, or create any scene you want.

If you already have a path that leads nowhere, don't rip it up! Put a bench, swing, or old-fashioned glider at the end of the path and give it a reason to exist.

A path is utilitarian. I have narrow paths of stepping stones in the middle of my flower borders so I have a place to walk and weed without stepping on the plants or compressing the fluffy flower-bed soil. The stepping stones are like a plant fertility clinic. Everything loves to seed itself between them. Many plants neurotically refuse to seed themselves anywhere else. I pull them out or leave them, according to fluctuations in my maternal hormones.

The simplest and least permanent path is made of wood chip mulch. It's a good medium to use if you are not sure where you want to put paths permanently but want to experiment to see where they will work best. Mulch paths are excellent in veggie gardens, since the ground under a mulch path will often become richer and be in better condition than the earth in the garden bed as the wood chips break down. Every couple of years, plant the vegetables in the paths and make new paths where you grew the vegetables before. It's a home version of the ancient agricultural practice of leaving one fallow field, a form of crop rotation that's important to organic gardening.

A mulch path looks neat and very "done" when outlined with two-inch-high lumber or brick edging. The edging visually separates the path from the surrounding plantings and keeps the wood chips from getting kicked around the immediate area. For a less "done" look, I use wood chips without edges as a way of keeping weeds out of the walking area in what I laughingly call my woodland.

Sally McCabe of Philadelphia Green told me that they use brown cardboard packing boxes instead of expensive wood chip mulch to make paths in converted city lots. Brown cardboard is thick enough to discourage the toughest urban street weeds. Because of its inoffensive light brown color, it's hard to tell what it is once it starts to break down into compost. Depending on the weather conditions, brown cardboard can last a whole season.

How to Lay a Permanent Garden Path

1. Using one-foot sticks and two parallel lengths of string, make an outline of the path. Ideally, a garden path should be at least four feet wide. That's enough room for two close friends to walk arm in arm and to allow plants to spill luxuriantly over the path without getting stepped on.

Tony Del Lago, a friend of mine who has a tiny garden at the back of a brownstone in Greenwich Village, knows lots of tricks, and some of them pertain to gardening. To create the optical illusion that his garden is bigger than it is, he set the strings farther apart at the front of the path near the house and closer together in the back. This creates the illusion of perspective, like the railway tracks you had to draw in art class in high school, where the tracks appeared farther away because the distance between the lines was narrower. It looked as if the back wall was much farther away than it really was. To further enhance the trompe l'oeil, he planted elephant ears with their enormous leaves in the foreground and specimens with smaller and smaller leaves toward the back. He also set a regular size watering can in the front of the path and a toy watering can at the back. At the very end of the path against the wall, he had an arbor only four feet high. The first time I saw the garden, I exclaimed, "Tony, how fabulous! It looks so big!"

He blushed at the compliment.

"How did you do it?"

He told me, and now I'm telling you.

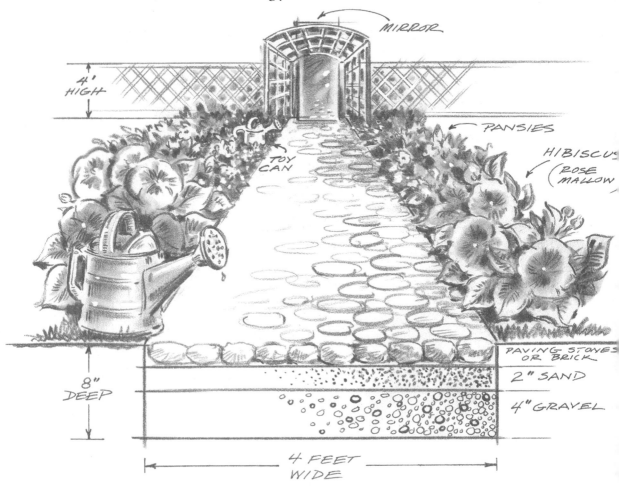

2. Dig out the path to a depth of eight inches and fill with four inches of gravel. Above that, put two inches of sand. If only sand or only gravel is available, you can use one or the other. The purpose of the sand and gravel base is to keep water from sitting under the paving stones once they are in place, causing them to heave and thaw in winter.

Whoa, hold it. I just told you I would dig a four-foot-wide path, who knows how long, to a depth of eight inches, haul off the soil, and fill it with tons of gravel and sand. See, now that's just the kind of advice I hate in gardening books. There is no way Walter or I would do that. That's too much work. Let me change that advice. Just remove a few inches of soil and fill with two inches of sand or gravel. That's good enough. In fact, if you live in an area with sandy soil, or in an area that doesn't have severe winters, forget the digging. You only have to take out enough to place your stones or bricks even with the surface.

I know what you're thinking: "Hey, wait a minute, Cassandra, how can I take your advice seriously if you keep changing it out of laziness?"

My gardening advice is always serious, but, you may have noticed, it is often inexact and approximate. There are a couple of reasons for this. In the first place, garden conditions are so variable around the country that I can really only testify to what has worked for me. And second, I don't think gardening should be so difficult and precise that the average person will be discouraged.

The truth is that good gardening is as improvisational and rewarding as good parenting. Sometimes those who seem to do it with the least effort get the best results. It annoys the hell out of me. So go ahead and dig the drainage layer as deep and perfect or as shallow and imperfect as you want. So you won't have a path that lasts forever, so what? Nothing lasts forever.

3. Rake the sand smooth. Place stones or bricks on the sand bed, butting them up against one another as neatly as possible. Work ahead of yourself, kneeling on the finished path as you go along.

When using paving stones of irregular shape, place the longest, flattest side along the edge of the path to keep the line straight. Use the largest stones at intervals, then fill in with the smaller ones. I like to fill very small areas with pebbles, seashells, or shards of broken dishes or pottery that I save for that purpose. You don't mind breaking a dish if you know it's going to wind up in the garden path.

To prevent the path from coming out wavy, use a spirit level and check that little green bubble every so often to keep all the stones on the same plane. If you are making a crazy-paving path using an eclectic variety of stones, they will be of uneven thickness. Adjust the level by adding or removing the sand under the stone.

There will be unavoidable gaps where oddly shaped stones do not fit together perfectly. In that case, you must either take a hammer and chisel and become a stone mason to fit them together tightly or you must fill the spaces with top soil and plant herbs, alyssum, creeping sedum, or other suitable plants. Yes, of course weeds will grow between the stones even if you fill the gaps with pebbles, but that's the price you pay for charm. A crazy-paving path does require more maintenance than a cement walk. But it looks fabulous with forget-me-nots springing up here and there.

Recently, a garden "expert" who shall remain nameless came to my house on a tour, and he said, "Oooh, I love the way those forget-me-nots randomly spring up between the cracks!" I knew then that he was a fraud. Random shmandom. Any real gardener would have known that it takes hours of sitting or squatting your way down the path, yanking up all the plants that are not forget-me-nots to achieve that casual look.

In truth, my crazy-paving paths only take a couple of hours to weed. When I'm ready, I turn the hose on and flood the cracks with water. The weeds pull out very easily, roots and all. There's a chance that the desired plants will float away as well, but if they do, I just stick them back in. Yes, I am sitting in a puddle, but there are worse things in life than a wet rear end. On a hot day, it's extremely pleasant.

4. Rest and refresh yourself that evening. After everything—the stones, bricks, crazy paving, and the gardener—have been beautifully laid and look radiant, you are ready for the last step.

5. Shovel builder's sand or earth over the path and sweep away the excess. If you prefer to have a solid path with no plants coming up in the cracks, sweep dry cement across the path and then water it in with a fine spray. When it dries, you'll have cemented the stones together.

I know this seems like a lot of work. It is. Think of it as an exercise program. And you'll have more to show for it than slightly thinner thighs. Hardly anybody will notice your thighs, but you can be sure they will notice the beautiful, artistic paths in your garden and admire you for them.

Arbors, Gates, and Other Transitional Features

An ancient garden gate was literally a door in a stone wall that could be locked, just as you might lock the front door to a house. As you may recall from the Errol Flynn movie, Don Juan had to climb the garden wall because the gate of the *jardin* of his inamorata was locked. The locked gate was therefore a metaphor for the lady's chastity, or more euphemistically in the MGM version, her heart.

A high gate still says keep out, ring, or knock if you want to come in, but like virginal movie heroines, you seldom see them anymore. A waist-high gate in a picket fence is friendlier, but does require the suitor to pause to open it instead of just traipsing in on the first date. This is a good metaphor for my cousin Helen's love life.

I don't want to carry this idea of garden gate as sexual metaphor too far, because I'm about to talk about archways, and according to psychologist Carl Jung, an arch is a female symbol the way the Washington Monument is a male symbol. But we are speaking about garden architecture here, and such digressions are distracting.

The garden arch is not only a very old architectural construction, it is a lovely, inviting shape, as we can see in such Gothic cathedrals as Notre Dame—which means Our Lady, by the way. Female.

An arch is a psychological entrance. Far from separating the rooms of the garden, a nice arch invites you to come in. Stop it.

A garden seen through the frame of an archway seems enchanted and begs to be explored, and if the arch is covered in flowers or leaves, so much the better. I mean it, cut it out.

Garden arches can be made of wood, metal, stone, topiary hedges, or specially pruned trees. An arch planted with wisteria, rose, clematis, or other substantial vine can transform an ordinary yard into a great garden just by itself.

More dramatic than a single arch is a series of arches that cover a walkway. It is the garden equivalent of the vaulted ceiling in the cathedral.

We are not going to talk about that anymore.

Where to Put Transitional Features Like Gates and Arches

Since a gate or arch defines the boundaries between garden rooms, the most obvious place to put one is where you enter the garden from the outside world. In fact, one of the nicest ways to privatize the front yard for those of us who don't have the nerve or desire to enclose it completely is to place a vine-covered arch at the end of the front path where it meets the street. Even without a fence or wall surrounding your property, an arch in that spot will declare that this front yard is no longer part of the "public park."

Another place to put a garden arch is around the front door. It turns the tract house into a cottage "with roses round the door" and looks as cozy as an old song.

Putting an arch between the driveway and the house is a pretty way to get to the car. Even better, plant a hedge between the car park and the garden. A car is not a garden ornament, although to see how many people keep cars in their front yards, you'd think they were sculptures by Rodin.

The simplest, earliest arches consisted of a couple of stone pillars supporting a cross beam, like Stonehenge. Although a twenty-foot boulder construction would make a powerful statement, I think such an arrangement might go beyond the boundaries of "informal" and enter the land of "nuts." If the house is in a part of the country where rocks are common, however, by all means use rocks. The difficulty with acquiring stone structures is not finding the stone, but finding someone with the skill and strength to build them. How many people besides Mel Brooks's 2,000-Year-Old Man know how to build a stone arch anyway? Good stone masons are rare and expensive.

Evolving from the Stone to the Iron Age, we observe that metal garden structures are about as permanent as rocks, especially if you cement them into the ground. Wrought iron, used for either plain fencing or fancy grillwork, is also durable and expensive.

Arches made of metal piping can be bought from garden supply catalogs, and they are very nice and reasonable, considering how long they last.

You can also make garden structures from the materials at hand. Years ago in Brooklyn, my neighbor Carlo made a strong grape pergola out of used plumbing pipes, which he connected by using the plumbing joints themselves. Afterward, he painted it with some iridescent purple enamel he had left over from the time he touched up the fins on his '62 Merc. I don't think he intended it, but it had a trendy high-tech look. I can visualize that iridescent purple pergola made of plumbing on a Southampton estate owned by a nouveau riche Hollywood mogul. Painted black or dark green, however, those pipes would be practically invisible when covered with vines.

For a more cottagey look, lacy wooden structures made of fancy carpentry or treillage are romantic and look like Victorian confections. These can be purchased at most garden centers or through catalogs. Most people paint them white, which is okay, but I prefer them painted in old-fashioned nineteenth-century earth tones, with the details picked out in shades of brown, green, gray, and Tuscan red, the way they are in Central Park in New York City.

HOW TO MAKE A RUSTICATED ARBOR

The only cost-incurring items you'll need for this work of art are a hammer and nails to knock it together, a drill, and a power saw to cut the pieces. If you can't borrow a power saw, or it makes you nervous, a pruning saw will work as well; it will just take a little longer to make each cut.

1. You'll need four saplings with trunks two to four inches thick. If you don't have weed trees in your yard, as I did, you'll have to buy lengths from the lumberyard or ask a neighbor who has a woodsy patch if you can him help thin it out. He might even be grateful. Cut the saplings into ten-foot logs. These will be the supporting legs of the arch.

Decide how wide you want the arch to be and cut two branches longer than that so the ends extend over the top, forming a TT. If you want to be even more artistic, fit curved branches together to make a Gothic arch top.

You also need eight one-inch-thick branches to brace the uprights. Each should be one foot long.

2. Nail the pieces together, using three-inch or four-inch nails. (To avoid splitting the wood, Walter used a drill to make a starter hole before hammering in the nail.) We want to form a four-legged structure with two legs on each side of the opening. First, connect one pair of uprights using the foot-long braces, then the other pair. You should use three braces for each side. Use two braces to connect the parallel top cross beams to each other. Once all the parts are together, nail the top to the uprights.

3. With a friend's help (it's heavy), carry the structure to its final location. Mark where the post holes will be.

4. Lay the arch down and dig four holes eight inches wide and two and a half feet deep. You might want to use a post-hole digger for this: If not, you'll have to make the hole wider just to get it dug. The depth is the most important part.

5. Line the bottom of the hole with six inches of stone, gravel, or sharp sand for drainage. The idea is to keep the legs from standing in water and rotting. Set the legs into the hole. Then fill in around the sides with more gravel or stone and finish with earth, and you're done. The arch will now stand eight feet tall.

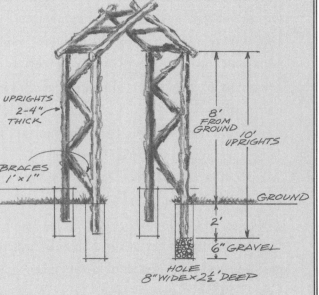

UPRIGHTS
2-4" THICK

BRACES
1" x 1"

8' FROM GROUND

10' UPRIGHTS

GROUND

2'

6" GRAVEL

HOLE
8" WIDE x 2½' DEEP

Rusticated structures, made of branches and logs with the bark still on, are unpretentious, and free.

I described how Walter built a rusticated arch in my previous book, *Mrs. Greenthumbs: How I Turned a Boring Yard into a Glorious Garden and How You Can, Too* (Crown, 1993), but it is so simple and cheap, and I'm so sure that anyone can do it, even me, that I will give the recipe here (see previous page).

There are variations on the basic arch, depending on how far apart you place the legs or how tall you want it to be. If you wish to make a seven-foot arch, use nine-foot uprights.

Sometimes a bench is strung between two of the legs. This is called a lych-gate, a covered arch wide enough to accommodate seats. If you put the legs far enough apart, the structure will turn into a pergola, but more about those later.

Easily the most popular choice of plant to dress up any arch is the rose. What is more romantic than a rose-covered archway? It attracts weddings like flies, and we and Carl Jung know why.

Roses aren't the only plants that can be trained over an arch. Any sort of vine can be used, and I mean *any*. When I first put up the rusticated arch in my garden, the first thing I planted was a climbing Queen Elizabeth rose, which promptly died. I felt hurt and disappointed, as one does when rejected by a love object. But once I freed my mind from the fixed idea that the only arch worth having is rose-covered, a whole world of interesting substitutes presented itself. The first year I planted blue morning glories, which were spectacular. The rose had hated my slightly alkaline soil, but clematis loved it, so I planted three kinds: *Clematis* x *Jackmannii,* a purple; Ramona, a blue; and Nelly Moser, a pink. The combination keeps color on that arch through most of the summer. Some high-style purists might suggest that I should have planted different varieties of the same color, all pink or all white, but I didn't think of it. I suppose that's one of the reasons I'm only Mrs. Greenthumbs and not a high-style purist.

A garden arch is a great opportunity to explore the entire exciting world of vines and climbers. Annual vines, such as nasturtiums, sweet peas, and the aforementioned morning glories, give instant gratification. Viney vegetables, such as scarlet runner beans, peas, and squash, make surprising and even amusing plantings. Ornamental gourds trained overhead look like strange sculpture, but be careful: If they get too big they can fall off and give you quite a bonk on the noggin.

A tree or shrub can be trained over an arch by pruning. Garden writer Rosemary Verey has designed a tunnel made of golden chain trees (*Laburnum anagyroides*) trained over a series of metal arches at Barnsley House. When in bloom the bright yellow wisteria-like flower clusters (a close cousin to that purple-flowered vine) hang down like yellow grapes. She has planted large purple alliums with round lollipop heads along the path underneath the arbor. I saw a picture of it all blooming together, and the purple and yellow combination was delicious.

Pergolas and Loggias, Gazebos and Belvederes

Many people confuse pergolas with loggias, and gazebos with belvederes. Many more have never heard of any of them. A loggia is a roofed gallery attached to the side of a building, like a narrow porch. A pergola is an openwork arbor or covering for a walk- or passageway. Since Roman times, pergolas and loggias have been used as outdoor dining rooms in warm weather, the way we use a sundeck to have barbecues. Unlike a sundeck, however, the area under the pergola is usually paved with flat stones, tiles, or gravel, and overhead vines shade the table and chairs.

As their romantic names imply, pergolas and loggias are common in Italy. Lucky Lombards, Tuscans, Romans, and Neapolitans have always eaten outdoors under pergolas and loggias. In Brooklyn, you can still find Italian-Americans, like my neighbor Carlo, sipping wine under grape arbors in the backyards of their brownstones.

When Walter and I bought our house, we found a strange slab of cement in the middle of the garden. It was about eight feet square and had originally been used as the base of a small structure, sagging pieces of which could still be found in the immediate area. At first, we assumed this was the ruin of a gazebo, a small open garden house which also has an Italian name and should not be confused with a belvedere, which is a gazebo that is placed to look out over a particular view. (*Bel vedere* means

"beautiful view" in Italian.) The more we learned of the biography of the previous owner, the less likely it seemed that he would have a gazebo. We found out later it had been a pigeon coop.

After we cleared the debris, our friend Jim Miles brought over some cedar posts and slapped together a pergola, using the cement slab as its base. It looked great. I painted the cement an unobtrusive dark brown and planted grape vines at the corners. In the twelve years since it was built, Walter has had to shore up the structure a couple of times, but the vines have done beautifully, and, with just a little spring pruning, produce seedless grapes every September.

The eight-by-eight-foot slab is just the right size to accommodate a table and chairs. On summer evenings after a long day of gardening, I feel Italian. I put Puccini in the cassette player and order a pizza. If you've ever had dinner al fresco under a pergola in the pink sunset of a long hot summer afternoon, you have partaken of the sweet life, or as we say in Rome, New York, *la dolce vita*—especially good with a nice chianti.

There is no reason why a sundeck can't be made into a pergola. All you need to do is erect an open wooden roof across the top of the deck and plant a substantial vine to grow on it. Grapevines are the classical choice, but if you can't grow grapes in your part of the country, try wisteria, trumpet vine (*Campsis radicans*), bougainvillea, or honeysuckle, among many others.

THE THIRD ROOM

In my half-acre yard, I have made the third room into a wildlife preserve, because it is the farthest from the house. I call this area Mother Nature's Garden, because frankly, Mother Nature is the only one who tends it. When I first started my garden, I regarded this wild area as a reproach to my character, proof of my laziness. I told myself and everyone else that I would get to it eventually. I would talk about woodland garden projects and make plans for elaborate plantings of ferns, hellebores, and lilies. After twelve years it's still a fantasy, but with age has come wisdom. I don't care anymore. I like this overgrown "woods," and the birds do, too.

In a yard large enough to accommodate it, the third room, or the room farthest away from the house, is the perfect place for trees, water areas such as ponds and bogs, fens, shrubs with berries, weeds with seeds—in other words, a place for birds and animals. It is the wild area away from civilization, the spot the children will seek out when they get to be teenagers. If each suburban family had a twenty-foot wild area instead of lawn between the back of their yard and the back of the neighbor's yard, we would create miles and miles of habitat for birds and frogs and mammals.

A wild garden gives you the glow of knowing that you are being ecologically helpful. It also gives you the even brighter glow of knowing that you have an area of yard that you don't have to mow, weed, or pay attention to unless you feel like it.

The entrance to this area can be romantic, perhaps an arch leading to a path made of wood chip mulch or fallen leaves into the woods.

An uncultivated area is the perfect place to put an objet d'art. To those of us who live in American cottages, it is the most unpretentious place to put posh garden ornaments such as classical statues and stone urns. It is just the spot to put that plaster copy of *The Kiss* by Rodin, which might look out of place next to the driveway. The juxtaposition of inexpensive high art and untamed lushness is as dramatic and romantic as Grecian ruins. Even religious statuary, which is usually displayed in front of the house in what looks like a bathtub surrounded by plastic flowers or Christmas lights in season, would gain beauty and meaning in a natural setting. What is more conducive to a state of contemplation than a saint, a Madonna, or a Buddha placed at the end of a small woodland path planted with violets, campanulas, ferns, and fragrant white lilies, if you are ambitious enough to plant them? What profound thoughts come to us when we see the same religious object loitering on the front lawn under a street lamp?

A Word About Garden Ornaments

Like good garden furniture, well-chosen garden ornaments give gardens historical reference, artistic aspirations, or at least cozy homimess. We see them all over the countryside—cement birdbaths, classical sundials, Victorian gazing globes, Japanese teahouse ornaments, plastic flamingos, plaster gnomes, racist jockeys, ducks, deer, and, my favorites, those wooden cutouts of a gardener's behind. I look at those and see a self-portrait. "Yes, that's me," I sigh.

Walter found a large Greek urn—actually an amphora—in the landfill behind the Buffalo's Club parking lot next door. I'm not kidding. It's about three feet tall and made of very thick terra-cotta. Part of the bottom is missing, but the flaw makes it look even more like something you'd find among the ruins of Pompeii. We spent some time trying to imagine who in the world would throw away such a lovely object. Anyone who owned it in the first place would want to keep it, wouldn't they? So what happened? We spent the evening under the pergola, drinking and conjecturing. Perhaps the previous owner had bought it for its original purpose, transporting wine, grain, or olive oil in galley ships across the Mediterranean Sea (although it smelled okay). To this intrepid ancient, the missing bottom might have been a heartbreaking, as well as a potbreaking, flaw. Agamemnon sacrifices his daughter and throws the jar into the landfill behind the parking lot. It's mysteries like this that make gardening intriguing.

For garden design purposes, the most important part of the mystery was not the urn's provenance, but where to place it.

Don't forget that most discriminating of judges, the Human Eye. Objects should be placed where you want the Eye to look, because It will. Given a view of natural objects, such as grass, greenery, and trees, or a man-made object, the Human Eye will always stop on the man-made object first. This might be a throwback to early hunting days when signs of human life meant a rival tribe was nearby, a theory that has a nice anthropological ring to it, or it may just be that humans think that man-made objects are more interesting than natural ones.

With this theory in mind, Walter and I wanted to place this ornamental object where we wanted the Eye to look. We considered placing it at the end of the path to say, "Stop, look no further." We thought of putting the urn at the corner of a new garden area to say, "Look, turn here." If we had two urns, we could have placed them at the ends of a hedge to indicate an opening. The classic place to put a tall object such

as an obelisk or column is at the intersection of garden paths. We didn't think the urn was quite tall enough.

You don't have to place objects purposefully. Some people prefer a more bingo-bongo, modern, asymmetrical feeling in the garden. But we knew that wherever the object was placed, whether deliberately or randomly, that would be the first thing a person coming into the garden would see. So we had to place it carefully to look random.

We didn't want to put it near any other object, either. A large number of garden ornaments in one yard can be obnoxious, although if they are peeking out from under hostas and surprising you from among the ferns, the effect might be cute. Maybe too cute.

Incidentally, if you insist on having a lot of kitschy garden ornaments, have a ton of them. Four ducks is tacky. Forty is an important collection. Perhaps not so important, but something.

We walked around the garden imagining what it would look like from various viewing points. (I had to imagine because Walter moodily refused to lug the hundred-pound object from place to place.) Then we called our friends Jo and Don and asked them over to lunch. After a beer, Walter and Don set the Greek urn amid some wild-flowers at the corner of a mown path that led into the uncultivated part of the yard. The effect is subtle and, I hope, unpretentious.

Speaking of pretentious, the last place you should place an object is out in the middle of the lawn. I don't care if it's the Statue of Liberty—no, especially if it's the Statue of Liberty. We have one on the lawn outside the Liberty Paint Store in our town and it looks like what it is: an advertising gimmick. A garden ornament is not supposed to serve the same function as the golden arches. It's not a display ad.

The irony of most garden ornaments is that the more they are obscured, the better they look. Any object will look well placed if it relates to something else nearby. Even cheap flamingos make more sense when placed by a pool where they appear to be fishing than they do starving to death on grass.

I prefer placing ornaments in such a way as to blend into the landscape. If an object is beautiful, it will look better framed by overhanging trees or flanked by foliage. If the object is ugly, silly, out of place, or made of plastic—and you know who you are—you will be doing a kindness to us all if it is placed so that it is half or, preferably, completely hidden among the daisies. Or in the landfill behind the parking lot. I know just the place.

The most useful garden ornament since Monsieur Rolex made the sundial obsolete is the birdbath. Birdbaths add the element of water to the garden, which highly respected garden designers consider not only desirable but essential.

My favorite place for a birdbath is in the middle of a sunny flower border. The heavy solid object makes a wonderful visual contrast to the light curvaceous flower blossoms. Birds enjoy the warm sunshine on their feathers as they bathe and stay around to partake of the nourishing nosh of seeds and insects that are close at hand.

Depending on climate, a cement or crockery birdbath must be taken indoors in the fall because frozen water will crack the basin. Birdbaths can be kept clean with a quick scrub of a brush and a rinse to get rid of the gunk on the bottom.

Enclosure of Large Yards

By the end of this chapter, I think it will be pretty obvious that I've been talking about suburban yards, from one-quarter acre to an acre in size. Commercial agriculture and orchard management don't come under the purview of this book, and the owner of a three-hundred-acre estate will obviously have different proportions and uses for the land than I do. Estates with a staff of gardeners maintaining rolling hills of park-like landscape suitable for riding to hounds have their own requirements, which need not concern us here. But for middle-class individuals with large yards of one to three acres of land, it is too much work to turn them into an endless succession of garden rooms.

I'll tell you what I'd do if I had one to three acres of land. I would enclose a quarter- to half-acre near the house for my flower and vegetable cottage-garden rooms, and I would divide the rest of the land into one-third meadow and two-thirds wild woods. I might help these woods along by removing some weed trees, like ailanthus and Norway maple, and planting native ones. (I probably wouldn't be too strict about this, however, and if some junk trees got in there, I would probably ignore them. The reason I know this is because that's exactly what I have done in my own yard.)

The "wild" area is a terrific place to put a meadow.

What About Those Meadows in a Can?

Sure, you can buy the can, but you won't get the meadow. I made a "meadow without the can." All I did was plant hundreds of spring bulbs under the backyard lawn and Walter stopped mowing it once a week. For about five years, all we got was long grass, but I was patient. It takes time for a lawn to turn into a natural meadow, I told myself.

Walter cut the long grass once a year. In areas that are naturally forest, like our yard in upstate New York, a meadow must be mowed once or twice a season to keep young trees from taking over. In the Midwest, a meadow grows after a prairie fire, so I was happy I didn't have to do that. Eventually, I lost patience with the long grass all summer, yanked out some of the more boring varieties, and plugged in perennial wildflowers like meadow rue, aster, goldenrod, and any weedy thing from the cultivated garden I wanted to get rid of. That's all I did to create a meadow. Walter mows paths through it and around it. Not only do the mowed areas facilitate walking to and from the rest of the yard, but the straight, clipped, obviously human touch makes the messy growth look like art.

Starting a meadow from scratch is another story. As I mentioned, there is no such thing as a meadow in a can.

Last spring, I learned a lot about meadow gardening for my cable television show when we went to Austin, Texas, to do a segment on Ladybird Johnson's brainchild, the National Wildflower Research Center.*

According to the man at the National Wildflower Research Center, the proper way to start a meadow is to plow the area just as if you were going to plant a field of corn, rake it smooth, and kill all the existing seeds in the ground by using herbicide. A non-

---

*Mrs. Johnson is well known for her work in restoring native plants, but in the 1960s she was a woman ahead of her time. When, as First Lady, she began her "Beautify America" project, she was ridiculed mercilessly. When she wanted to restore urban parks in Washington, D.C., she was told that poor people don't need posies. How dare she waste federal money on flowers along the highways when there were people starving in the slums? And the Russkies didn't waste money on nature stuff, why should we?

Mrs. Johnson stuck to her guns and roses. Now everyone agrees upon the important and incalculable effect of green spaces in urban environments. The goal of protecting and restoring the American landscape is high on the list of national priorities. And the Russians have some of the most horrendous environmental problems on the planet.

chemical way to do it is to cover the entire area with clear plastic. The unwanted seeds will germinate, then cook to death under the intense greenhouse-like heat. Once the ground has been sterilized in this way, you then sow the proper native plant seed mix for your area. If you write to the people at the National Wildflower Research Center, 4801 LaCrosse Boulevard, Austin, TX 78739, they will be happy to tell you what that is. At the Research Center, they use native species only! Any plant that came here after Columbus is a *flora non grata* and is promptly yanked out.

We also visited Wanda Fielder (what a great name for a wildflower lover) who put the meadow into practice. You should have seen her Texas bluebonnets, Indian blankets, and daisies all blooming in what used to be her front lawn. She admitted that making the meadow was just like flower gardening for the first year; she had to weed and water the meadow religiously to make sure all the plants were well established. But since then, she has given it no fertilizer or extra water. For the last three years, she has done nothing except to enjoy the view and cut the flowers for bouquets.

For those of us who are not purists about native wildflowers, or who live in a less marginal environment, making a flowery meadow doesn't have to involve complete destruction of all existing vegetation. We can adopt the method I learned from Christopher Lloyd.

MY FIRST CHRISTOPHER LLOYD STORY

My Christopher Lloyd is not the talented character actor who appeared in *Back to the Future* and *Taxi*. Mine is one of the great gardeners of the twentieth century. He is generally credited with inventing the mixed border, where shrubs, perennials, annuals, herbs, roses, even trees are planted all together with the emphasis on color, texture, and form. We take this style of gardening for granted today, but in the 1920s and 1930s, it was a radical departure from the standard carpet bedding of Victorian England.

Mr. Lloyd is a member of the second generation of great English garden designers who had their flowering in the early twentieth century. Gertrude Jekyll, Vita Sackville-

West, Lawrence Johnston, and Russell Page, among others, were the pantheon of great ones whose books made me want to be a gardener.

Mr. Lloyd was the first of the famous English gardeners I interviewed on my ten-segment TV Grand Tour, and the only one on the aforementioned list of greats who is still alive. You can imagine how thrilled I was to meet him.

We drove to his home, Great Dixter, in Kent, which is south of London. Even the name seemed exotic to me. The only previous connection I had ever had with Kent was when I used to buy Kents with the Micronite filter before I gave up smoking.

Mr. Lloyd is of medium height with beautiful white hair and a matching William Powell mustache. The morning I spoke to him, he had a well-worn (perhaps too well-worn) suit jacket on his slightly stooped shoulders. He asked if his clothes were all right for the camera. They were perfect—he looked like an eccentric English gardener, and he knew it. In an antic moment, I offered to change into an evening gown with opera gloves and tiara if he would put on white tie and tails. He declined to change, but he did say that my bright red lipstick was quite festive enough. This was a man who appreciates color and beauty, I thought to myself. For the rest of the afternoon, I flirted with him like mad. To no avail.

Christopher Lloyd has a meadow instead of a lawn in front of his medieval manor house. When I came upon it, it looked like an ancient "merrie mead" and a hip lawn alternative dreamed up by the Green Party, all at the same time. Actually it is both. It was started by Mr. Lloyd's mother before World War I. She was a good friend of the Gertrude Jekyll set. (Imagine! I was making eyes at a man who had known Gertrude Jekyll when he was a boy.) This group of gardeners was responding to the destruction of the nineteenth-century English countryside in the same way we are concerned with the American landscape today.

In March and April, the meadow was full of daffodils, which Mrs. Lloyd had started from seed. Other spring bulbs included crocus, guinea hen flowers (*Fritillaria Meleagris*), giant snowdrops (*Leucojum aestivum*), and dogtooth violet (*Erythronium dens canis*). In May, it featured camass (*Camassia Quamash*), an American native that also does well in England (what doesn't?).

Mr. Lloyd insisted that a successful meadow should be sunny and have poor soil. Like the Texas wildflower people, he said the less you improve it, the better. He mows his meadow in late winter, to give a head start to the early spring bulbs, then again in late July after the summer flowers have gone to seed and the bulbs have finished ripening off.

His mother's flowery mead was so successful, he turned much of what was a formal English lawn into meadow as well. Instead of resting solidly on perfectly manicured greensward, a series of topiary sculptures now seem to float on a waving sea of color and undulating grass.

Mr. Lloyd doesn't make a meadow by plowing up the area and starting from scratch, as was done in Texas. He has no interest in sterilizing the soil to remove foreign seeds. He recommends that you simply stop mowing for the first summer, just to see what comes up. In my case it was grass, but what you get will vary according to climate and geography. Then cut the grass very, very short (one to two inches) in early autumn. (Remember, all meadows must be cut at least once a year anyway to retard tree growth and keep long grasses from shading out flowering plants.) Add bulbs and perennial plants right into the turf. In spring, Mr. Lloyd rips up long patches of grass and plants annuals.

Yes, he does have to grub thistles and other noxious weeds out of the meadow from time to time. Did I mention that Mr. Lloyd runs a commercial nursery at Great Dixter and has a well-trained staff of brilliant, dedicated gardeners at his command? Even his head gardener, Fergus, has become famous. We who are without Fergus can still maintain a pretty good meadow, but I must admit he would be fun to have around.

Look, I realize that to many readers the whole idea of completely rethinking your landscape seems strange, revolutionary, and a lot more difficult than mowing the lawn. Maybe you think I'm eccentric, obsessive, or worse, stupid. But I'm suggesting a new way of arranging the yard. Or rather, an old way of gardening, before the invention of the power mower. It does not require more work than the present method of "extreme gardening," just different work. With enclosures, meadows, and trees, you have control over those parts of the garden that are cultivated, and you have very little fussing with the rest. I think this type of gardening is ecological, cheap, and very pretty.

PLANT PERENNIALS AND PLANT THEM ABUNDANTLY!

FOR MOST OF US, gardening is not our primary occupation—
if only it were! If only I could do it professionally, I used to say
to myself, and make money at what I love to do for free.

Let me tell you something, my friend, some things are better done for free. And I
don't mean only the obvious thing. I had much more time in my garden before I went
professional. Nowadays I spend much of the spring and summer traveling around the
countryside talking about gardening with precious little time to work on my own. So
be careful what you wish for, my friend.

I know I'm not alone in having only a little time to garden because of work, family,
etc. It is a common problem, but I have a solution! I use plants that fill the yard without constant watering, pruning, spraying, etc. I use plants that will come back every
year by themselves, so I don't have to buy them and plant them every spring. I use
plants that will make more of themselves, so that the only work they require after
planting is to be cut back or divided every few years!

I'm talking about perennial plants, my friend: trees, shrubs, and herbaceous
perennials—flowering plants that grow back from their roots every year. Most of us

are familiar with these plants and have at least some of them in the yard. But as I have traveled around the countryside, I have noticed that something is missing. Most people have a few perennials, but the gardens still look mingy and stingy because they lack two important qualities: abundance and proportion.

ABUNDANCE

Look at the Sistine Chapel by Michelangelo. More conveniently, look at the picture of the Sistine Chapel provided on the following pages.

It's full. Did Michelangelo paint it white and put a saint in the corner reading a book? No! He filled the space—God creating matter out of Chaos, seven Hebrew prophets, five sibyls, rosy-cheeked, muscular boys wearing garlands, the Deluge, more muscular boys! He put moldings between the different segments to give it all form. The moldings serve to separate each part of the design the way that a fence or structure separates the parts of a garden. Notice how the characters seem to overflow the heavy separations of the ceiling's design, like plants and flowers growing over the confines of a garden fence or wall.

The Sistine Chapel is full of color and nude figures, two elements that are assets to a garden as well.*

---

*A lot of people have wondered at all those nudes in what is supposed to be a religious painting commissioned by the pope. Even such an eminent expert as H. W. Janson, in his famous *History of Art* (New York: Prentice-Hall and Harry N. Abrams, 1962), the textbook for thousands of college art courses, speculated on the many "garland-bearing nude youths that accompany the main sections of the ceiling":

> These wonderfully animated figures play an important part in Michelangelo's design . . . yet their significance remains uncertain. Are they images of human souls? Do they represent the world of pagan antiquity?

Was Mr. Janson born yesterday?

It doesn't take the Sistine Chapel ceiling to fall on my head to see that Michelangelo put all those figures of handsome young men in the chapel ceiling because he was crazy about them! You think Pope Julius II was concerned that Michelangelo's lifestyle would upset family values? Or that he had a "don't ask, don't tell" policy concerning the artists that he commissioned to paint the walls?

Renaissance Italians were not prudish Victorians or straight-laced Puritans or members of the Legion of Decency. The Rome of Michelangelo's time resembled the dissolute Rome of the Caesars far more than the pious religious center of the present day. We would find the behavior of the Renaissance popes scandalous.

Julius II, the pope who commissioned the Sistine Chapel, was a man of furious temper and constant cursing. He was a warrior pope: he went to war with Bologna and reinforced his attack by first excommunicating his enemies and then granting a papal indulgence to any man who would kill them. In the Renaissance, celibacy was loosely interpreted to mean "never legally married," and he had at least three illegitimate daughters, although he wasn't as loving a father to them as Pope Alexander VI was to his daughter, Lucrezia Borgia (that's another story).

To his credit, Julius II was one of the greatest art patrons who ever lived, and a ceiling full of nudes would hardly have offended him. On the contrary, the fact that it illustrated stories from the Old Testament was Michelangelo's idea!

Besides being the source of interesting footnotes, the paintings in the Sistine Chapel teach us a satisfying aesthetic principle. What the Sistine Chapel has—in abundance—is abundance. Abundant life bursting the boundaries of confinement is joyous—it is practically the definition of joy. Such a creation is more than something out of nothing, it is the triumph of everything over nothing, the chorale at the end of Beethoven's Ninth Symphony, the overflowing cornucopia, the Nile at high flood.

Unlike the figures on the ceiling of the Sistine Chapel, garden plants will not only *seem* to burst out of their boundaries, they will. Plants will grow over supports, fencing, pathways, even furniture unless kept in check. Maintaining the balance between the geometric lines of the man-made structures and the lustiness of the living material is called gardening, our occupation and our art.

More Abundance

There are those who prefer spare architecture, refined art, symmetry, control, order, stasis, death. I respect that, but I don't like it. Life, which is what we are dealing with in the garden, is never static. Life in the garden is never orderly without the tyrannical rule of iron in the form of clippers, lawn mowers, hedge shears, loppers, saws, etc.

I prefer a garden that is full and slightly wild, but innocent and pure, like a painting by Henri Rousseau. I like it to look as though its stems and flowers were never sullied by the cold touch of steel or the noisy violation of chain saw and mower, as though everything beautiful just happened to have grown there by chance.

Of course, this is a lie. To make a garden appear both natural and aesthetically pleasing, you must clip unsightly or spent flowers, shape shrubs so they don't overwhelm one another, weed like mad, and most important of all if you want everything to look random, plant carefully.

How to Plant Carefully to Achieve Abundance

Where to plant that peony is a decision, but it is not a moral one (unlike the decision whether to sleep with that married man next door, for example). If you make a mistake in the garden, you can fix it with a shovel.

Now we are ready to ask ourselves, how much is too much? My motto is: More is more, less is stingy, but don't obscure the boundaries too much or "more" will turn into "mess."

Massing Plants

I don't know why, but we all do this. We go to the nursery, fall in love with five or six plants, and bring them home. Then we put one plant over here in front of the house, the other one over there, a third in the back, a fourth next to the porch—you get the idea. Pick a spot! Put them all together! Organize them into groups. One daylily from the nursery is not going to fill in the front of the house. However, one daylily in front of a euonymus bush next to a couple of black-eyed susans next to a peony is the beginning of a pretty good garden.

Planting in Drifts

Many people plant flowers in two ways. They place them in shapes like a paint-by-number kit, or they plant as though they were designing a checkerboard:

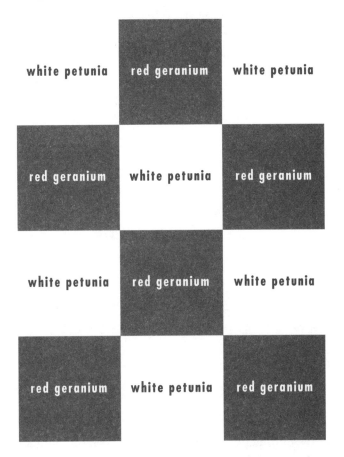

. . . seeing it in the garden is as boring as reading it on the page.

My neighbor Ross always planted this way and it drove me crazy. Every July, he would buy flats of annuals on sale at the local nursery, an act of thrift of which I approved. Then he would ask me for advice about how to arrange them in the little flower bed near his front door. I'd spend my precious gardening time arranging his plants in pleasing color combinations, keeping the marigolds away from the hot pink petunias, putting the taller salvias behind the shorter periwinkles. Then I would go away and leave the act of planting to Ross. The next day, there they were, inevitably planted in rows, the shapes and colors neatly interspersed with one another, looking like ducks in a shooting gallery.

"You probably don't like this style of planting," he would venture, noticing my stony silence, my glare, my utter disgust. "But it looks neat."

Of course he'd think it was neat. His aesthetic sense was developed at the age of eighteen in the armed services during WW II. What is lovelier than parade formation?

"General MacArthur would be proud," I'd snap, and go off fuming. This happened more than once. I suspect I was being unkind, and I'm sorry now. Gardening was a great pleasure to Ross, and was the only exercise he was allowed to do with his bad heart.

But even annuals really do look nicer if you plant them in clumps, especially large clumps of plants of one variety. That is the way I had arranged Ross's flats. It would have looked good from a distance because it allowed each of the bright annual colors to make a big splash.

HERBACEOUS PERENNIALS, THE QUEENS OF THE GARDEN

As Michelangelo might tell you, formal, geometric garden spaces combined with abundant plantings have intrinsic drama. There is a theatrical tension between the straight lines of the garden structures and the flowers, fruits, and leaf patterns that burst forth out of the boundaries of the design. It looks fabulous and is very liberating psychologically.

One way to achieve this look is to plant perennials in drifts. A drift is a number of plants of the same variety planted in a wavy or S-shaped line.

For some reason, plants look better when they are planted in groups of three, five, nine, twelve, and fifteen. Don't ask me why; all the experts say so.

This means that when you are starting a garden, it's better to plant a lot right away. It helps to have a lot of money so that you can afford to buy at least three of everything to start with. ("Have a lot of money" is the subtext for most of the horticultural advice I read in gardening magazines.)

If you don't have a lot of money, buy one perennial plant and let it grow for a year or two until it's big enough to divide into three or even five smaller specimens, then replant in drifts.

The great perennial gardener Gertrude Jekyll was one of the masters of drift planting. In addition to being an author, she was a professional horticulturalist who installed gardens from scratch for wealthy nobility who demanded (and got) instant gratification. When planting a flower border, she put the tall plants in the back row as you might expect, but brought one or two plants forward. Then she drifted shorter plants in front of the tall ones, a little to the left or right of the first drift. A third group of shorter plants went on the other side of the tall drift, with a few plants in front of

the second drift. In that way, it looked as though the plants were weaving in and out of one another, just as they would do in nature.

She said the reason she did it this way was so that there were no noticeable gaps in the flower border as the perennials came in and out of bloom, a lapse that would have piqued her clients.

Planting in drifts rather than in rows or clumps will make the border appear natural and well established instantly. But anyone who has had a garden for more than a couple of years will tell you that even if you plant a perennial border in rows like a corn-field, after a few years the plants will find their own way around the garden and all your planting schemes will be shot anyway. When that happens, wise gardeners say to their friends, "Yes, my garden has really 'come into its own.' It's so mature now." The idea of letting the garden go its own way will be discussed in chapter 3, "Use Plants That Grow Easily in Your Climate and Location."

Packing the Border

"Packing" means planting perennials over bulbs for a succession of bloom. I first read about packing in a book by Vita Sackville-West, another one of those old Brits. She's the one who called it "packing," but the technique itself must be older than that, since Vita lived in the twentieth century and it's difficult to believe that no one ever did it before 1935. (As a kid, I believed no one ever did "it" before 1968. But I digress.)

Vita Sackville-West had her own method of packing, but this is my version: It is suitable for use with almost any type of spring bulb except daffodils, because ripening daffodil leaves tend to flop over on their neighbors and will smother the plants around them. Crown Imperial fritillarias, Asiatic lilies, Oriental lilies, or tulips are a good choice if you live in an area without deer, but if the deer little darlings eat your garden the way they do mine, plant allium bulbs. Deer won't eat alliums because they're related to the onion, which is repellent to nonhuman mammals.

1. Dig a hole eight to ten inches deep and as long and wide as you need to plant the larger bulbs. Six to twelve per planting hole is about right.

2. Throw in some compost and set in the bulbs, then fill the hole with more compost and soil to about four inches from the top. Now put in the smaller early spring bulbs, such as crocus, miniature daffodil, Siberian squill (*Scilla sibirica*), or a combination of several varieties.

3. Before you fill the hole, plant a summer-blooming perennial, such as daylily, yarrow, campanula, etc., on top.

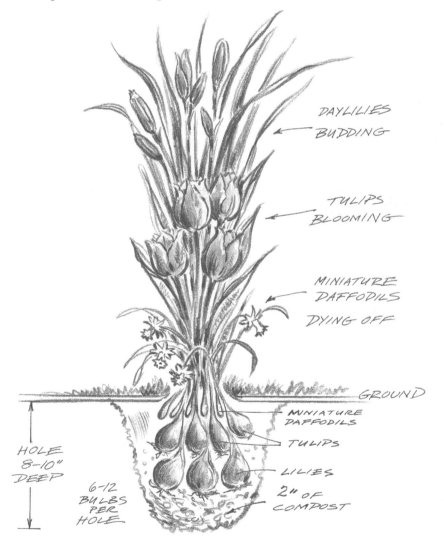

DAYLILIES BUDDING

TULIPS BLOOMING

MINIATURE DAFFODILS DYING OFF

GROUND

MINIATURE DAFFODILS

TULIPS

LILIES

HOLE 8–10" DEEP

6–12 BULBS PER HOLE

2" OF COMPOST

The result is spectacular. The crocuses bloom in early spring, then the tulips, allium, and Crown Imperial fritillaria in late spring. When the spring bulbs go brown and ripen off, the emerging leaves of the perennials mask them. In June, the Asiatic lilies bloom, coming up through the leaves of the summer-blooming perennial. Just as they finish, the perennial will start to bloom. When the summer perennial is past it, the Oriental lilies are just getting started.

The secret to success in packing is plenty of rich compost in the planting hole. One hundred percent compost is not too much. Use thick mulch, which will continue adding humus to the soil as it breaks down. Some bulb food, sprinkled over the soil once a year, wouldn't hurt, either.

I pack my garden using all sorts of combinations. Just the other day, I planted white Asiatic lilies under columbines. The bloom times of the columbines and the lilies overlap slightly, but in such a lovely way!

Dividing Perennials

Of course, the easiest way to get lots of plants for free is to divide up the ones we already have. The beauty of most herbaceous perennials is that they can be dug up and pulled apart into separate little plants, then replanted in drifts of five, twelve, or five hundred, depending on the size of the clump we had to begin with.

A lot of gardeners I know (my friend Bobbie) absolutely hate to dig up a beloved perennial and commit surgery on it, either by pulling it apart or (brutally, according to her) cutting right through the root ball. It's understandable. Division is a form of asexual reproduction. While most humans are crazy about sexual reproduction, they find the idea of asexual reproduction somewhat revolting.

Plants whose leaves arise directly from the roots, like hostas, daylilies, delphiniums, columbines, Japanese anemones, astilbes—most herbaceous perennials, in fact—are thrilled to be divided. If they could, they would beg for it. In nature, an herbaceous perennial finds new soil by adding new plantlets next to itself each year. Eventually, a bare spot develops in the middle of the clump where nothing grows. Seen from above, the newly sprouted plant looks like a balding man. If left in one place too long, herbaceous perennials will use up the nutrients in the soil, cease thriving, and sometimes they will stop blooming altogether. Such a plant would like nothing better than to be lifted entirely and pulled or cut apart into many pieces and replanted in fresh soil.

Those English gardening books I used to read when I first started gardening insisted that you must have the gardeners dig up the entire perennial border every two years, an instruction I found very difficult to follow.

In their rarefied world of perfect horticulture, gardeners would leave the plants out on the lawn while they carefully dug over the earth and added fresh compost and manure from the stable. Then they would divide and replant the perennials in the same place they were before so as not to spoil the garden design, which was probably by Gertrude Jekyll.

I lack a staff of gardeners. The idea of digging out a hundred feet of border, leaving the plants cooking in the hot North American summer sun while I kill myself shlepping wheelbarrows of compost (I also lack stables) and double digging it all into the soil is beyond my comprehension, not to mention my physical ability. Or even Walter's physical ability. In reality, I only attend to a perennial when it stops blooming altogether or has become so puny it seems in danger of dying out completely. This condition is known euphemistically as "running out," the New Age horticultural equivalent of "walking into the light."

I would like to say that the plants in my garden never "walk into the light," but that would be a lie. However, the vanished ones have mostly been new introductions that were unsuitable to the particular conditions of my yard. How did I know they were unsuitable? They dropped dead, fast, that's how.

If a plant looks puny because a more aggressive plant has broad-shouldered it out of the way, I will pick up both of the plants like naughty kittens, dig up the area of battle, and replant them on more equal terms. But, as I say, I don't do this too often.

There are a couple of tricks to easy division of perennials. You can leave the whole plant right where it is, but take a piece or two off the side, using a sharp spade to cut through the crown. Then you can replant the little divisions nearby. It takes longer to get really big drifts this way, but you'll have less anxiety about mangling the original plant. This method also works if you are acquiring a plant from someone else's garden—with his permission, of course. It is illegal to take a plant without the gardener's permission, even though a little piece off the side will hardly ever be noticed, especially if it is taken in the middle of the night.

The secret to success in starting little transplants is to make sure each division has lots of roots. The leaves are not as important. A division can have its leaves damaged, but if there is a good crown of roots, the plant will send up new leaves right away.

After divisions are planted, water them well and keep them out of the broiling sun for a couple of days. Don't try to hasten things by giving them fertilizer, which may burn tender damaged roots. I have roots on my red hair, and I assure you, chemicals do those roots a world of good, but I'm not a delphinium. A cool rich root run with plenty of water is all the fledglings need.

SHRUBS, THE QUEENS OF THE PERENNIAL GARDEN

A low-maintenance garden is made up of shrubs. That's the reason you see shrub collections planted in front of hamburger stands, shopping malls, and medical centers all over the country. As soon as the blacktop is dry in the new strip mall parking lot, a team of "landscapers" plant the "island beds." They truck in topsoil, shrubs, throw down some black plastic, and cover the whole thing with pine bark mulch. No further maintenence is required until a couple of the rhododendrons turn yellow from chorosis or die from lack of water. Such "landscapes" require no mowing, which we know is the most labor-intensive part of gardening, and little weeding and watering, thanks to the mulch. They also require no imagination whatsoever.

Personally, I love them. A shrub border is a good idea even when badly done by evil people. A well-executed planting of handsome shrubs is a tremendous asset to a private house. The size of a shrub is in much better proportion to a house than most flowering perennials, and it does not overwhelm it like a large tree does. Shrubs last for years. They are the pillars of the garden, its sovereigns, its queens. They provide substance and shelter. They make the garden more interesting. If you've ever played in the bushes as a child, you may remember the pleasure of finding a secret hiding place under the billowing skirts of an old spirea.

A border of flowering shrubs is like a flower border, only bigger. The great advantage is that you can cover a large amount of ground that you don't have to mow or weed, and you still get flowers for the house.

How to Plant a Flowering Shrub Border

STEP 1: Cover the entire area with newspaper mulch. Newspaper mulch is my favorite. Back in the old days, double digging a garden was considered a necessity for three very good reasons: It cleared the earth of thick sod, of weeds or grasses that no other plant could penetrate, it softened hard, compacted earth so that the roots of small plants could breathe and establish themselves, and it was a way to add nutrients and texture to soil that needed it. Gardening books said you had to dig down at least a foot to make all of this happen.

For most of us, this meant we had to confine our flower and vegetable beds to the area we had the energy to dig. Instead of the glorious postcard cottage gardens of our imagination, all we could manage was a one-foot strip along the house, or a tiny vegetable patch in a sunny backyard corner. And if we were more ambitious, it meant renting a rototiller or a back brace, whichever came first.

I have discovered a method for making compost, eliminating weeds, and softening the ground without digging or rototilling. Let me repeat that in caps: WITHOUT DIGGING OR ROTOTILLING. I call it "The Old Newspaper Trick." I first read about this technique several years ago in an article by Nancy Carney in *Fine Gardening* magazine and I have been using a version of it ever since.

"The Old Newspaper Trick" works well for any type of garden. I covered my entire vegetable bed with newspaper, then dumped autumn leaves over it and left it there all winter. Then, in spring, I brushed aside what was left of the leaves, took a pair of scissors, and cut away enough paper to make a row two inches wide. Then I planted my seeds as usual. After the seeds sprouted, I put a fresh layer of newspaper between the rows, and I never had to hoe. I was amazed at how efficiently the newspaper kept watering down to a minimum. Best of all, I have never had to dig or rototill my vegetable garden again. I swear.

a. Select a spot where you wish to plant a flower bed, a shrub border, or a vegetable patch. In this case we are planting shrubs. But it doesn't matter how much ground you have to cover, because you don't have to dig it up! You don't even have to clear it! It doesn't matter if grass, weeds, or brambles are growing on the spot; you're going to go right over them. Take old newspapers over to the area. Use black-and-white newspaper, not the shiny paper. Newsprint ink is made of lampblack and oil, and biodegrades easily. Full-color newspapers like *USA Today* or supermarket tabloids will do, since they contain soy-based dyes.

b. Now spread sheets of newspaper over the area the way you would place a tablecloth over a table. Lay them out flat on the ground, four sheets thick, and let the edges of the sheets overlap each other by three inches. If you are covering a particularly tenacious weed, like poison ivy or crabgrass, make the newspaper ten or twenty sheets thick. The idea is to keep all light from reaching under the newspaper. This lack of sunlight will, of course, cause the weeds, grass, or whatever else is growing underneath to die, which is exactly what we want. This is the same idea as the clear plastic, except that our aim is not to sterilize the soil, but to make it break down into humus.

c. I know what you're thinking. Who wants to look at old newspapers lying all over the garden? Let's face it, twenty feet of newspaper spread along the side of your front walk is unattractive. It doesn't look so hot to the neighbors, either, especially if a high wind comes along and whips the stuff into their yard. They might get angry at you, even without the high wind, and who can blame them? The newspapers look like garbage and the headlines are depressing. So, the hardest part of this labor-saving method is to spread leaves, weeds, wood chips, or other organic material over the newspapers to cover them and keep them from blowing away. This cover of wood chips and clippings does not have to be deep, just thick enough to hold down the papers and hide what's underneath.

d. Time is now your ally (for a change!). Leave the newspaper alone for about six months. If you have laid out the newspaper and the wood chips in the fall, by the following spring the area will be ready for planting. Everything under the newspaper will have turned to compost—stems, roots, and all—along with some of the newspaper and the organic material on top. The newspaper, like any other porous mulch, also keeps the soil moist while allowing air and water to pass through, thereby keeping the area soft and aiding in the breakdown of the plant material.

e. Now you can just brush the mulch aside and cut or tear a hole in the newspaper, and plant into soft, rich ground. To be sure that your new plants have a perfect start, you may want to add extra compost or manure to the hole at planting time. In subsequent years, add more newspaper and wood chips between the plants to discourage weeds.

If you are planting a shrub border that is fifty feet long and twelve feet deep, this will take a lot of newspaper, but you can save up. Most communities have a newspaper recycling day. Watch for it and grab those bundles before the trucks arrive. Then cover the newspaper with wood chips, leaves, clean straw, sea kelp, or any other mulching material that is cheap and plentiful enough to obtain by the truckload, and you are in business.

So far we have done the same thing the shopping mall "landscapers" do when making their shrub borders, except that we are using newspaper instead of black plastic.

STEP 2: This is the fun part. Wait and plan. Over the winter, while the grass and weeds are being broken down into compost under the newspaper and mulch, look up the vital statistics of your favorite shrubs. There are many excellent books on the subject, and good catalogs can be a gold mine of information. Bad catalogs can be a minefield of misinformation, but more about that later.

Find the ultimate height of each shrub variety so that you can plant the taller ones in back and the shorter ones in front. Check the blooming times to have something in flower throughout the gardening season. Find out about their favorite growing conditions, such as whether they prefer acid or alkaline soil, sun or shade, wet or dry conditions. Cut out pictures of shrubs from the catalogs and put them next to one another to create artistic color combinations. Talk to gardening friends to find out what has worked best for them and to beg a few suckers from their bushes.

Like herbaceous perennials, shrubs look better when planted in drifts of three, five, or nine. If you are covering a very large area, twelve of one type of shrub is not too much.

For example: To cover an area fifty feet long by twenty-five feet deep, it will take approximately five large shrubs, such as lilacs, in the back row; six medium-size shrubs like weigelas in the middle; and twelve small shrubs, like Russian sage or potentillas, in front, planted in drifts, of course.

Purchasing a large number of shrubs at one time is very expensive, but there is a way around that, which is to take divisions from the shrubs you already have. Like taking divisions from herbaceous perennials, taking shrub divisions is a non-kinky form of asexual reproduction.

25 FEET

50 FEET

FIVE LARGE LILACS GROW UP 15 FEET

SIX MEDIUM WEIGE[L] GROW UP 8 FEET

TWELVE SMALL POTENTIL[LA] GROW UP 4 FEE[T]

Some shrubs are really small trees that grow from a single stem, like the star magnolia (*Magnolia stellata*), the witch hazel (*Hamamelis*), and the rose-of-Sharon (*Hibiscus syriacus*). But many shrubs grow from multiple stems that emerge directly from the ground, like the bridal wreath spirea (*Spiraea arguta*), quince (*Chaenomeles speciosa*), forsythia (*Forsythia intermedia*), lilac (*Syringa*), mock orange (*Philadelphus*), and many more.

Multistemmed shrubs can be divided with a sharp spade, a pair of loppers, and a pruning saw. I have often taken a few stems with roots attached from off the side of an existing shrub that is growing in a friend's yard and replanted it in my own, without injury to the plant or the relationship. Except that once . . .

STEP 3: Plant. Remember that the little shrub in your hand is only two feet high and two feet wide today, but it may eventually grow to ten feet high and ten feet wide. To allow for their ultimate size, you must leave several feet between the plants. Yes, it's true, a newly planted shrub border is a pathetic sight, with two-foot-tall plants spaced six feet apart. The way around this is to buy large shrubs right away, if you can afford it, or to plant herbaceous perennials, ornamental grasses, or small shrubs in between.

You can then remove these plants as the shrubs fill in. Architectural annuals like cleomes don't even have to be removed as the shrub grows. They will be shaded out.

The cruel truth is, while the shrubs are getting bigger, you will be getting older. But the older they get, the less work shrubs require! The older you get, the less work you'll want to do. (So you and nature mature very well together.)

It's so difficult to project yourself into the future. The kitten becomes a cat. The baby becomes a teenager. The two-foot forsythia you planted next to the kitchen door in 1984 is now a big bush that hits you in the face when you go out, in the backside when you go in. Of course you must either cut it back or move it, which is tedious and difficult (see "How to Move a Shrub," chapter 1).

The way to prevent this common tragedy is to plant shrubs as though they were already the height and width you intend them to be. Plant the shrub at least six to ten feet from the edge of the path. That will leave a big empty space at first, but again it is a pleasure to fill that space with flowering plants while waiting for the shrub to grow in.

How to Thin a Shrub

If it's too late for prevention, then the overgrown bush must be dealt with surgically. The common way to keep a shrub in bounds is to cut back all the branches to make it smaller, resulting in the well-known formal topiary gumdrop. This is a familiar sight, giving modest gardens all over the country that "This is Versailles! Isn't it? Oh, *yes* it is!" look.

Perfectly clipped shrubbery is dignified, and topiary is an ancient and honorable horticultural technique, but I don't think a yard full of topiary is suitable for cottage gardens.

Since Roman times, topiary was displayed in the gardens of the wealthy because it was an example of conspicuous consumption. Like lawns before the age of lawn mowers, clipped hedges, manicured knot gardens, and fanciful floral animals had to be maintained by the handiwork of a large staff of servants. The topiary garden was a refined way of saying you could afford to hire a large number of people or, in more ancient times, own them. Nowadays, topiary has lost its social cachet. Nowadays, all it means is that you can afford to buy electric hedge shears at Home Depot.

In a cottage garden, a couple of clipped shrubs strategically placed among the informal plantings give structure and contrast. Too many clipped shrubs are pretentious and, unless faithfully maintained, look like bad haircuts.

An inconveniently large shrub is an eyesore and a nuisance, however, and you have to do something. I keep shrubs in bounds by thinning them. This consists of removing the longest branches at ground level. To do the job, I get down on my hands and knees with the clippers, the loppers, and the pruning saw and crawl under the bush. First I clean out the leaves, dead branches, and miscellaneous garbage. You'd be amazed at the junk that collects in the middle of an old shrub. Then I shake the branches at the bottom to see which ones are the longest ones. Sometimes you can tell by following the branch with your eye, but once you are in the thick of it, so to speak, shaking is the way to go. Walter came out of the house while I was doing this one day, and it took him a long time to figure out why the spirea seemed to be waving at him.

Cutting out the first few branches doesn't seem to make much difference, but as I continue to remove the longest branches, the shrub gets smaller and smaller, as though time were reversing itself. The change is subtle and dramatic all at the same time. Not only have I reduced the size of the bush, but I have admitted light and air to the center, encouraging vigorous young growth. The bush is rejuvenated! It looks ten years younger and no one can figure out why. Would that I could do the same thing for my body.

TREES, THE QUEENS OF THE PERENNIAL GARDEN

That's right, trees, shrubs, and herbaceous perennials are all queens of the perennial garden. Guess who's the servant.

Trees can be planted in large drifts and massed together in groupings in the same way as other perennial plants. The famous eighteenth-century "natural" English landscapes by Tradescant and others were really massed groupings of trees and large shrubs set against lakes, rivers, and rolling green hills. Because these landscapes were meant to be viewed at a distance, trees and masses of shrubs were the only plantings large enough to make the picture work. Flowers and other floral details were lost in the green and blue of distance.

When the American suburban version of the English landscape was first applied, the public park ideal included trees in the sea of clipped grass. You may have noticed that early suburbs from the 1900s to the 1930s, like Long Island's Great Neck, or Ladue in St. Louis, are shady places with tree-lined streets and tree-filled front yards. After World War II, however, suburban houses were built on smaller and smaller lots and builders were less careful about (and probably ignorant of) the public park ideal. Building contractors would erect a house, sell off the topsoil, and throw down a carpet of sod as an afterthought. Trees were not planted at all by the developers of tract houses.

Generally, the more upscale the community, the more trees it has. Trees add grace to a suburban landscape, no doubt about it, but personally, I envy the person who bought from a cheap developer. They have the opportunity to put the trees where they will do the most good.

While trees are invaluable landscape features, *don't start a cottage garden by planting a tree.* Full-size or even dwarf fruit trees are an asset around the perimeter of the area, but don't put one in the middle or you'll be buying books on shade gardening in a few years. Too many big trees make gardening a struggle for light.

In a small yard, and I'm talking about a half-acre or less, the useful place to plant a large tree is on the west side of the house. A deciduous tree will provide cool protection from the hot afternoon sun in the summer, and in the winter it will politely shed its leaves to let the warm afternoon sunshine in.

We Americans have an almost religious feeling about trees. We even have a tree-planting holiday, Arbor Day, which I love and support, but planting trees in a small cottage garden is stupid, and I'm not the only one who thinks so.

In the 1950s, Norman Taylor was to suburban American gardening what Dr. Spock was to suburban American children, the most consulted expert of the time. He was the author of *Taylor's Garden Guide*, editions and versions of which are still read today. He gave this advice in 1957:

Where to plant . . . shade trees . . . will be dictated by the size of your frontage, how far back from the sidewalk your house stands and whether or not there are any trees planted between the sidewalk and the curb. . . . If there are existing street trees and the house is less than thirty-five feet from the sidewalk, *it is better to omit all large trees* [italics mine]. Hedges, small trees, and shrubs can be used instead, to give another kind of permanence and thus avoid the smothering effect of the street trees plus one or two of your own.*

I like that phrase "the smothering effect." Anyone who has tried to grow flowers under a maple tree will understand perfectly. If only more people had taken his advice! If only more people had taken Dr. Spock's advice!

In other words, whenever possible, large trees should be used on large properties, small trees or shrubs in small yards.

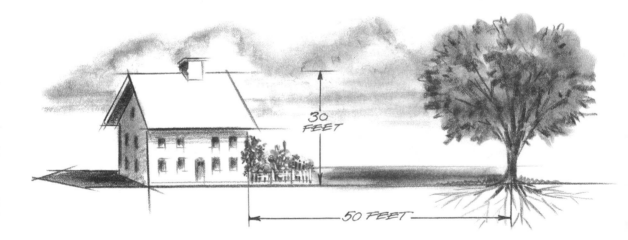

*Norman Taylor, *Taylor's Garden Guide* (Princeton, N.J.: D. Van Nostrand Co., 1957), p. 52.

If I had a choice, I would never plant a tree closer than fifty feet from my house. If I had a yard that was smaller than a quarter-acre, I would not plant any large trees at all, but stick to big shrubs or dwarf trees. The important phrase in this paragraph is "if I had a choice." I didn't have a choice.

Because I bought an old house, I was stuck with trees in inconvenient places. There were plenty of weedy ones in the yard. I had no compunctions about removing them or "taking them out," as the gangsters say. Walter and I completely cleared all the trees out of two large garden rooms, but left all the shrubs.

There was one magnificent elm at the far corner of the yard. It was easily three stories high and, miraculously, healthy. Of course, I left it, along with a stand of weed trees.

I admit, it is unfair to use the term "weed tree," since in the right place a weed becomes a specimen. I'm referring to trees that flourish in disturbed soil and seed themselves with all the gusto of an army bent on rapine. I was "blessed" with fine "specimens" of honey locust, ailanthus, ash, ailanthus, sumac, ailanthus, and maple. Because the stand of trees was at the back of the yard, all I did by way of gardening was to plant a couple of oak trees. I called it the wild woodland garden. This area is now the third garden room of my yard, as I wrote about before.

If this nonchalant approach seems too simple to you, remember that this is nature we're dealing with here. You don't have to knock yourself out to make it look good. That elm and that little woodland is lovely all by itself and makes a dramatic contrast to the cultivated gardens.

Unwanted Trees: A Random Sampling

What do you do when you have some big trees that were planted by fools who never read Norman Taylor forty years ago and your yard is now a dank, mossy dell better suited to a grotto than a colorful cottage garden?

It's hard to say. I'm not sure I would have the nerve to "take out" a forty-year-old Norway maple, although I'd be tempted to. My neighbor John did, but only after lightning hit it. As a general rule, I would recommend removing a tree that was not rare or very old if it was in the only area where I could put my garden. But in practice, this decision is not so easy. Those big trees have character. They grow on you, and over you. And everything else.

To help solve this difficult conflict, I asked six gardening friends of mine what they would do if the only place they had to garden was dominated by a forty-year-old Norway maple. I did not choose this particular variety of tree at random. I have a forty-year-old Norway maple in my yard. On the one hand, I can't help but love it.

In summer, its leaves obscure the vista of the Buffalo's Club parking lot, which otherwise would be seen from the second floor of my house. And I must admit, in the fall when the leaves turn bright lemon yellow, the thing is beautiful. Fortunately, it is growing near the driveway, on the north side of the house where I don't do much gardening anyway, and the roots only impinge upon a weedy area along the edge of the driveway pavement.

On the other hand, the tree is already bigger than my house and still growing. It releases thousands of seedlings, all of which germinate everywhere, so I am constantly pulling winged maple babies from the gardens and the paths, and cutting down surprise saplings that have insinuated themselves in the middle of the lilacs. If I had been starting from scratch, I would have planted smaller trees or shrubs along the fence. But I wasn't starting from scratch. Quite the contrary, I was starting from the big fat end.

But enough of my problems; back to the question: What would you do if you had a forty-year-old Norway maple in the middle of the garden? My comments are in parentheses.

Bobbie: "I have a tendency to like flowers." (Tendency? She's mad for flowers.) "But I have a fear of cutting something down that is older than I am." (I don't think a forty-year-old maple is older than she is, but I won't quibble.) "I feel this way: if it made the garden dank and dark—a lot of New York City gardens are dark, but they do wonderful things with ivy, you know—I guess I would take it out, but if it wasn't too bad, I would just plant ferns and forget about it." (She's a coward about cutting, dividing, or transplanting anything.)

Ken Slevin (my agent, a doll): "I had this very problem. I had a big maple in my yard and I took it out. Even though I loved the shade, the roots were screwing everything up. They were terrible. In dry weather they were coming right out of the soil looking for water. Nothing would grow there. Can you hold on a minute? [On hold] Okay, I'm back. Even now, after I took it out, when I tried to dig there to plant the bulbs you gave me. Hold on. (I gave him a dozen unusual daffodils as a thank-you gift. That's just the kind of client I am.) I'm back. I still had to wrestle with dead roots. It was so bad I had to go get the ax." (When my agent gets out the ax, beware!)

Mary, Queen of the Shady Garden: "You're talking about a maple tree, a forty-year-old maple tree? (She is very bitter about the deep shade in which she is forced to garden.) Oh, I sure would. Unless Granddad always sat under it and that was his favorite spot. In that case, I would wait until he died and then cut it down. If I had the money I would move the tree to the cemetery, or else mulch it and strew it over his grave, something sentimental like that. The stump would make a nice base for a birdbath."

Michael Gelman (television producer and avid organic gardener): "You've got to have respect for a forty-year-old tree. (Michael is in his thirties with lots of land.) I would leave it and garden someplace else. (He was reminded that there is no other area.) I'd find a way!" (I must introduce him to Bobbie.)

Pamela Jones (master gardener and author of *Just Weeds*): "As a rule, I recommend that you should try to save trees whenever possible. The decision to cut depends on the health of the tree. (I reminded her that this was a Norway maple.) Oh, well, if it's a healthy tree, you've got a problem. This happened to me twice and I cut down the trees. (She said this with no discernible regret.) But it took ten years for the roots to rot. (That she regretted.) Those maple trees don't die gladly. They fight. (She went on to design an instant small garden on the spot.) After the tree is down, it's still impossible to dig. I would put a container garden on top of the area, over stones or bricks or cinder blocks, and keep the whole thing at least four to six inches off the ground. Those maple hair roots will crawl right into tubs. That means you'll have to water often, but that's okay. In a small garden you don't have anything else to do anyway." (She laughed contemptuously. She makes huge gardens for wealthy people.)

Peter Bevacqua (ad agency executive and garden artist): "You mean if I had a forty-year-old maple tree and the only place I could put my garden was right under it? You're damned right I'd cut it down! Otherwise you have to plant everything in pots. Forget it. I'm not a container type of guy." (He's usually not this brutal.)

These were the uncensored opinions of six gardeners, selected randomly from the small number of people who actually speak to me on a regular basis. But I think their responses are typical of gardeners all over the country, and even if they aren't, the research budget of this project won't cover a national survey, so these will have to do. Frankly, I was shocked at the ruthless responses of these mild-mannered gardeners. Here is a perfect example of what I mean about gardening mayhem. This magnificent struggle with nature that we call horticulture will turn even the most civilized, educated, refined person into a tiger.

Thrilling, isn't it?

I am grateful that I can leave the large Norway maple next to my driveway, since I have plenty of other spaces in which to garden. For those who are not so fortunate, attack!

The problem with a large tree in a small yard is not only the shade, but the tree's size in relation to the yard. Things are out of proportion. It is an example of the other element we must consider when planting perennials. . . .

5'4"

PROPORTION

The Parthenon pictured here is an example of Greek classical proportion. The proportion is the relationship between the width of the temple and its elevation. For two
thousand years, artists have agreed that Greek classical proportion is the spatial relationship most pleasing to the human eye.

Architecture is not the only field where this proportion works. Luckily for us, Greek
classical proportion is useful for planning garden structures and borders as well as Grecian temples. Using a formula, it is easy to figure out how wide to make a border flanking a path, or what to plant in relation to the front of a house. The formula is:

TWO TO ONE PLUS ONE (2:1 + 1)

In the garden, that means that the shorter item is half as long as the longer one, plus
one more foot. This sounds complicated, but it's really very simple, like everything
else once you understand it.

Let's say, for example, your house is twenty feet tall. What is the ideal size for the
shrubs in the front yard?

TWENTY-FOOT HOUSE: 20:10 + 1 = 11-FOOT SHRUB (OR SMALL TREE)

Using Greek classical proportion, the tallest plantings in the front of the house
should be eleven feet tall.

Wow! That is much taller than those foundation plantings you see in front of suburban houses all over the countryside. That explains why they look so skimpy. They
are out of proportion to the height of the house.

Wait a minute. No one wants eleven-foot foundation shrubs. Common sense tells
us that a shrub eleven feet tall would obscure the front windows and damage the foundation. So plant the eleven-foot shrub eleven feet from the house to give it some space.
Place it to the side, at an angle to frame the house, then plant the area between the
eleven-foot shrub and house with shorter shrubs and perennials, leaving the shorter
plants to decorate the foundation. The house would then be set snugly into the land-

scape, framed but not overwhelmed, in classical proportion to the surrounding vegetation.

Bad proportion is the reason why the ten-foot lilac is not flattered by a row of petunias planted in front of it. Using the proportion 2:1 + 1, there should be a six-foot shrub in front of a ten-foot lilac.

TEN-FOOT LILAC: 10:5 + 1 = 6-FOOT SHRUB

It's common to see a row of pot geraniums or other small annuals planted along a picket fence. You can tell that in her mind's eye, the person who planted it was thinking of something along the lines of a charming cottage garden. But alas, the row of geraniums is out of proportion to the fence.

Using Greek classical proportions, 2: 1 + 1, if the fence is four feet tall, the flowers along the bottom should be at least three feet high.

FOUR-FOOT PICKET FENCE: 4:2 + 1 = 3-FOOT-TALL PLANTS

This formula also works well to determine how deep to make a border. According to the formula, the flower border along the fence should also be three feet deep.

Plantings along a fence or a wall often look wrong, and now we know why. A six-foot fence would be graced by a border that is four feet deep, and shrubs that are at least four feet high.

SIX-FOOT FENCE: 6:3 + 1 = 4-FOOT-DEEP BORDER

Proportion can also be used in reverse. You can make the object in proportion to the plantings instead of having the plantings in proportion to the object. In other words, a six-foot fence can have a ten-foot-deep border along its length.

TEN-FOOT BORDER: 10:5 + 1 = 6-FOOT FENCE

A generous, ten-foot-deep border looks fabulous in front of a six-foot-high fence. A few of the tallest plants could also be ten feet tall without completely obscuring the fence. Some people would think it's a little too big, but as Walter told me one enchanted evening, "a little too big" is a compliment.

The formula will be helpful when in doubt about how to arrange any type of plantings in relation to any structure. Even a kitschy object will look better with a flower border that is in proportion. Take the fake wishing well on the lawn. Please. Most people plant a row of annuals around the base and it looks dinky. A wellhead is usually about four feet high, not counting the cute peaked roof. At the very least, the border of flowers surrounding it should be three feet wide and some plants three feet high.

FOUR-FOOT WISHING WELL: 4:2 + 1 = 3-FOOT FLOWER BORDER

By the same formula, a three-foot-high birdbath should have a two-and-a-half-foot border around it.

THREE-FOOT BIRDBATH: 3:1.5 + 1 = 2.5-FOOT FLOWER BORDER

A birdhouse sitting on a post six feet high should have a four-foot border.

SIX-FOOT BIRDHOUSE: $6:3 + 1 = 4$-FOOT FLOWER BORDER

You get the idea.

Now it becomes clear why it looks as though we don't garden. We are out there planting like mad—we want to make a nice garden—but the borders aren't wide enough and the plants we choose aren't big enough.

A four-foot-wide path is in proportion with three-foot-wide borders on either side. This is much handsomer than the one-foot-wide border you often see along the path to the front door.

FOUR-FOOT-WIDE PATH: $4:2 + 1 = 3$-FOOT-WIDE BORDER

In my garden, I reversed the proportion and made the path smaller than the borders. In other words, I have a pair of six-foot-deep borders flanking a four-foot-wide path.

SIX-FOOT BORDER: $6:3 + 1 = 4$-FOOT-WIDE PATH

Skimpy, it's not. Planting in proportion is artistic, although its effect is not obvious. Very few people will walk by and exclaim, "Oh, what lovely proportions!" when admiring the landscape in front of your house, not like when they admire the flowers, the trees, or the gardener's behind. But everything will look better, and only you and I will know why.

Hold it! Hold it! I know what you're thinking. That's all very well about proportion, but here's just another gardening how-to book telling me to make two six-foot-deep borders flanking the path that leads to my house. But my house is twenty-five feet from the street. How the heck am I supposed to fill two six-foot-wide borders that run the length of the front walk? "Are you crazy, Mrs. Greenthumbs?" I hear you protest. "You think I'm made of inexhaustible money—or even more precious, inexhaustible time? Am I rich, immortal? If I wanted impossible fantasy gardening, I would be reading Martha Stewart, not you."

I swear it's not impossible. Remember what this chapter is about: perennials.

MAKING PERENNIALS, THE QUEENS OF THE GARDEN, DO THE WORK

The way to fill a large area is to use the right shrubs. When I began to plant the six-foot borders along the path to the front door, I took out shrubs that had been there for years, a mock orange and a lilac, because I thought they were too big. They had been planted too close to the path in the first place, and at fifteen feet tall, they were out of proportion.

After a couple of years, however, I noticed that the now all-herbaceous perennial borders needed more structure, substance, and height, so I began adding shrubs. This time I chose varieties that would stay a manageable size for a long time. For winter interest, I planted three holly bushes (*Ilex* x *meserveae* 'Blue Prince' and 'Blue Princess'): two princesses and a prince (a ménage à trois), which I have never seen grow taller than eight feet in my climate, and I will keep them pruned to about six feet tall if they ever grow that big. I also have flowering shrubs: an old-fashioned rose with simple white flowers (*Rosa alba*), white-flowered garland spirea (*Spiraea Thunbergi*), summer-blooming dark purple butterfly bush (*Buddleia Davidii* 'Black Knight'), a May-blooming red Chinese tree peony (*Paeonia suffruticosa*), and a yellow-flowering potentilla (*Potentilla fruticosa*).

Between the shrubs, herbaceous perennials fill large areas of the border. By now, I have fewer varieties of plants than I started out with, but those that remain have substance and authority. There are six very large clumps of white herbaceous peonies (*Paeonia officinalis*), four large drifts of white phlox (*Phlox paniculata*), and masses of red-flowered daylilies (*Hemerocallis*). Shorter perennials, such as lady's-mantle (*Alchemilla mollis*) and cranesbill (*Geranium sanguineum*), grow along the edge of the path as well as a few low-growing creepers like lamium (*Lamium* 'White Nancy'), sedum (*Sedum spectabile*), and sweet woodruff (*Asperula odorata*). Any spaces are filled by annuals such as alyssum (*Lobularia maritima*), cleome (*Cleome*), nasturtium (*Tropaeolum majus*), dahlia, canna lily, etc.

I try to repeat the same plant at intervals along the path. Repeating the same plant at intervals gives a nice professional look to flower borders. Repeating the same plant at intervals is very soothing. Repeating the same plant at intervals can be boring, however. Repeating the same plant at too-close intervals brings us back to my neighbor Ross's white petunia–red geranium obsession.

Repetition gives order and form to nature, however, and when done at odd intervals doesn't seem regimented at all. Repeating the same plant at intervals is virtuous in many ways. It shows you had the good taste and restraint to avoid buying everything you saw in the garden center, or that you had the enviable horticultural ability to divide and replant perennials successfully. It is also a sign of thrift, an admirable trait even in nongardeners.

One of my favorite examples of successfully repeating the same plants at intervals is the garden in Bryant Park, right behind the New York Public Library in the middle of Manhattan. The borders flank a large lawn, which is used for the public to sit and lounge upon during the day, and provides a bucolic setting for concerts in the evenings. This park is also the location of the New York fashion-industry shows every year, so its aesthetic value is very important.

The flowering borders are very large, and unlike many municipal plantings, which

are made up of bedding annuals, they are laid out as if this were the biggest cottage garden you ever saw. It is indeed a high-fashion, sophisticated cottage garden. Because of their large proportions, the borders contain shrubs as well as drifts of flowering perennials. Among the shrubs are purple-leafed sand cherries (*Prunus cistena*), which are eight feet tall with delicate pink flowers in spring, and variegated weigelas with dappled green and yellow leaves and pink trumpet-shaped flowers in summer.

These are accompanied by Russian sage (*Perovskia atriplicifolia*), a four-foot shrub with pale gray leaves that contrast beautifully with the purple leaves of the sand cherry. In summer, the Russian sage puts forth its almost-blue flowers as does the oak leaf hydrangea (*Hydrangea quercifolia*) with its giant cream-to-mauve flowery puffs and its architectural deep green leaves. Between and in front of these substantial shrubs are masses of perennials such as enormous, pink-flowered hollyhocks (*Althaea rosea*), large clumps of phlox (*Phlox paniculata*), drifts of deep red–leafed heuchera (*Heuchera micrantha diversifolia* 'Palace Purple'). The short heuchera with its rounded purple leaves balances and echos the purple-leaved sand cherry beautifully.

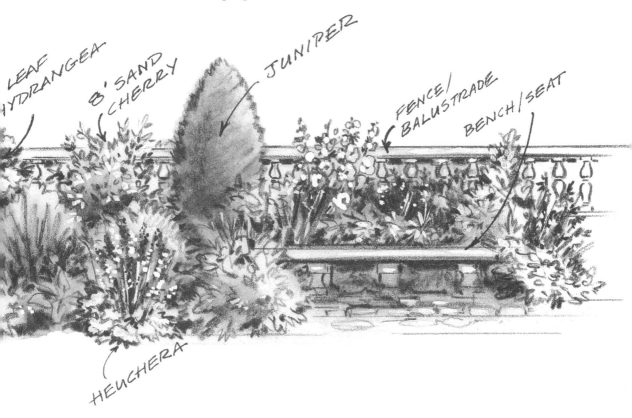

As you look down these borders, you get the impression of waves and drifts of color and form rather than regimented blobs. The main plants are repeated every twenty feet or so, establishing a pink-to-purple color scheme and an almost formal pattern without being too stuffy about it. I wish my garden were as well organized as this one, but I just don't have the discipline. A public garden like the one in Bryant Park is an inspiration, however, and an excellent role model for us private gardeners.

It's a shame, but often the only really elaborate gardens that the average person sees are those imitations of European royal *jardins* that surround public buildings and decorate public parks. You know the kind I'm talking about. You see them in front of county courthouses and historic landmarks all over the country, those beds of hothouse annuals planted to make fancy shapes or to spell out the name of the town. To many people, they represent an ideal garden, a fantasy to be imitated. Next to the signs that say, "Don't Walk on the Grass," I think public gardens should have signs that read, "Don't Try This at Home!"

Recently, I was sent to Niagara Falls by *Live! with Regis and Kathie Lee* to do garden segments from the public gardens on the Canadian side of the Falls.

Niagara Falls is big. We are talking about one million bathtubfuls of water falling 170 feet every second. Every second. It makes me feel clean just thinking about it. It is truly a breathtaking sight, especially from the Canadian side.

I wanted to do my segment in the parkland bordering the river, which was full of hardy trees and shrubs, along with some interesting perennial borders—all plantings that could be imitated in home gardens fairly easily. I wanted to show how it was done and why it looked so good. But since the rest of the show was being broadcast from a fancy-shmancy Italianate garden overlooking the Falls, I had to talk about that one instead.

It was just the kind of public garden I didn't want to advertise: a Villa d'Este hillside with stone balustrades and grand stairways suitable for a sword fight in *The Count of Monte Cristo*. The plantings were perfectly maintained with bedding plants such as canna lilies, tree-form lantanas, wax begonias, and dusty millers in perfect, weed-free formal designs.

In order to keep a formal garden like this looking its best, bulbs are planted in fall, then removed after they are finished blooming in spring, to be replaced by annuals, which have to be specially grown in greenhouses so that they're already flowering when they are set out. Sometimes a third change of plantings is necessary when plants brown off or get diseases.

This was a high-maintenance, expensive garden and the Canadians could afford it, I was told. Unlike the American side, which is funded by the government and is subject to fluctuations of revenues depending on whether the Democrats or the Republicans are in power, the Canadian park is self-supporting; the money made from tourism is used to maintain the park. So the Canadian park has lots of money, and it shows: acres and acres of park landscaping featuring rare and beautifully maintained trees and shrubs and wonderful perennial flower borders, as well as that royal *jardin* full of bedding plants.

"Don't do this at home!" I shouted over the noise of the Falls during my segment. "This takes twelve gardeners—full time!" Just then, a handsome Royal Canadian Mountie came on the scene, ostensibly to help me with the digging, but really because I had asked for him to liven up the segment. After the show I asked Brian (the officer's first name) if he realized that Mounties were considered to be sex symbols by many women.

"You bet. I get mobbed whenever I'm on park duty!" he admitted readily, and laughed, his white teeth lighting up his dimpled cheeks and ruddy face beautifully. He had blue eyes the color of a Canadian lake in springtime, and he was wearing a red coat and leather riding boots that . . . But I digress.

Where was I? Oh, yes. We see attempts to imitate the bedded annuals of public "palace" gardens all over the place. In a private yard it looks feeble—the little clump of petunias surrounded by dusty millers in a spare tire, the row of marigolds in front of the mailbox, the single row of celosia planted along the front walk, flanked by an acre of lawn. Pathetic.

Grand public gardens are to home gardens what Mounties are to husbands—they're fantasies. But why try to emulate a fantasy when the real thing is more accessible, more affordable, and, in my opinion, more beautiful in its own way?

My favorite spot in Niagara Falls park never got on the air. It contained a gravel path flanked by wildflowers leading to a rusticated gate that hung half open. Beyond the gate was a magnificent pink-flowered smoke bush (*Cotinus Coggygria*) that obscured the area beyond, inviting further exploration. "My husband could make a gate like that, no problem!" I said to myself. Here was a garden that could be maintained by someone like me, an ordinary middle-aged woman with a friendly husband at her command. The wildflower path would need only some weeding and a yearly mowing, and the shrub would need no maintenance at all. And with the money we'd save on all those expensive bedding plants, there's no law that says I can't buy Walter a red coat and riding boots. A little fantasy does have its place.

What better place for fantasy than the garden room? I know people who make butterfly gardens, specialize in one-color gardens, rock gardens, Shakespeare gardens, or rose gardens. I respect these people very much. Their gardens have a thematic and aesthetic unity that I find admirable.

I can't do it. I can't resist a pretty plant. When I see it, I want it, I buy it, take it home, and plant it where ever I can find a place. If I had a similar moral code when it comes to romance, I would be divorced several times over by now.

That is the reason I grow a cottage garden. I can stick everything in with complete abandon and no discrimination whatsoever.

The Disney Institute Garden

I did see a home-appropriate public garden on another television trip, this one to Disney World. The garden I admired was at the Disney Institute. When I first heard the name, Disney Institute, it made me laugh. What did they teach there, Goofy calculus, Mickey Mouse journalism? Actually, they really do teach horticulture. To the institute's credit, the teaching garden, where they give classes, looked exactly like the kind of garden I would make if I were setting out to teach home horticulture. First of all, there was no lawn. You can imagine how that warmed my heart.

The layout of the garden, really two garden rooms, was a perfect example of what to do with a typical suburban yard.

Two instructional buildings faced each other with walls connecting the two buildings so that they formed an enclosed courtyard paved with stones. In the center was a small water feature surrounded by potted plants. The fourth wall had a big arch with a very nice climbing red Don Juan rose. The arch led to the main garden.

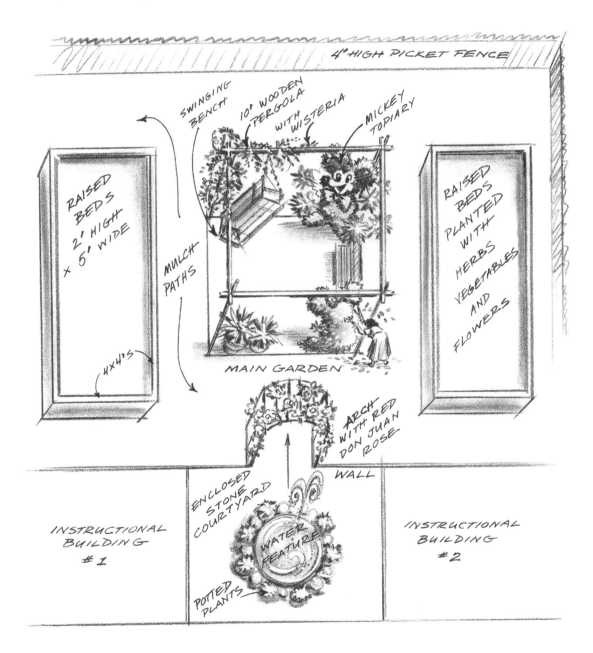

4' HIGH PICKET FENCE

SWINGING BENCH

10' WOODEN PERGOLA WITH WISTERIA

MICKEY TOPIARY

RAISED BEDS 2' HIGH X 5' WIDE

RAISED BEDS PLANTED WITH HERBS VEGETABLES AND FLOWERS

MULCH PATHS

4X4'S

MAIN GARDEN

ARCH WITH RED DON JUAN ROSE

ENCLOSED STONE COURTYARD

WALL

INSTRUCTIONAL BUILDING #1

WATER FEATURE

INSTRUCTIONAL BUILDING #2

POTTED PLANTS

As you passed under the arch, directly ahead was a large wooden pergola planted with wisteria vine. Under the pergola were benches, one of which swung from wires attached to the beams of the structure, thereby making the necessary place to sit. I sat there. There were pots of tropical plants all around the perimeter of the pergola, including several topiary sculptures of Mickey and Minnie and, I think, Pluto. These figures were appropriate to this garden, though perhaps not suitable everywhere.

To the right and left of the pergola were a series of long raised beds about two feet high and five feet wide made of treated four-by-fours. They were just high and wide enough so that the gardener could sit and weed the beds without bending over. These beds were generously planted with herbs, vegetables, and flowers; they had mulch paths between them and the whole area was enclosed by a four-foot fence. I would have preferred a higher fence for my yard, but, unlike private gardeners, the designers at Disney World wanted their garden to be visible from outside the boundaries.

The arrangement of paths and raised beds seemed to me to be perfect for the older gardener (which we will all be someday) or for someone with back trouble. As anyone who is familiar with French intensive gardening will tell you, a raised bed with enriched soil is also the perfect place for growing a whole season of vegetables close together and in rapid succession.

MORE WAYS TO USE PERENNIALS

Those of us with small yards are always looking for more places in which to plant. One of the most neglected areas in the neighborhood is that strip between the sidewalk and the street. In suburbs, this area is often the site of grass or trees. If you have a strip of grass between the street and the sidewalk and no trees are planted there, it can be an opportunity to do something creative.

A neighbor of mine, Elizabeth (Betty) Swanson, has a shady backyard—big, big maples behind the house—need I say more? So the only place she can grow flowers is in the front yard of her house, which consists of two four-by-eight-foot areas behind the picket fence on either side of the front path. But, lucky for her, she has no street trees. As you might hope, she has planted flowering perennials in her front garden, and they look beautiful.

But she really went to town in the two-foot-wide strip between the sidewalk and the street. There she has planted wildflowers. Actually, the word *planted* is inaccurate. She finds weeds she likes and encourages them by cutting the grass around them by hand with a grass clipper. She has voluntary Queen Anne's lace, black-eyed susans, violets, and coneflowers, along with some hollyhocks and blanket flowers she planted there herself.

Because there are flowers behind her wooden fence on the other side of the sidewalk, the curbside planting is a continuation of her little front garden. It looks great.

For the most part, the strip between the sidewalk and the street tends to be treated by most of us as though it were an embarrassment—an extra bit of earth we didn't intend to show, like underwear sticking out. Many people, including the previous owner of my house, just pave the whole thing over and create a double-wide sidewalk.

What a lost opportunity! I would like to suggest that we use the cement sidewalk as though it were a garden path, and the area between the path and the street as part of the front garden. If you live in an area that doesn't have a plant sale, the strip between the sidewalk and the road is the perfect place to stick those extra divisions of too-abundant perennials.

Often the area between the sidewalk and the road is planted with trees, in accordance with the previously mentioned grass-and-tree "suburbia as public park" concept.

I admire street trees very much. They clean the air, absorb traffic noise, and add class to uninspired architecture. I consider them a mark of civilization. Having said that, I realize that we no longer agree upon the definition of civilization, but never mind. In my opinion, civilization is having the time, the safety, and the values to create objects for the sake of beauty alone, and that includes planting and maintaining street trees.

Before the incursion of Dutch Elm Disease (I hate to capitalize a horrible disease; I prefer to capitalize things I like—Chocolate Mousse, French Kiss), magnificent elms were planted along the avenues of North America, their tall vase-shaped crowns meeting in the middle of the street to form Gothic arches as graceful as those of the cathedral of Notre Dame. Then the disease struck and denuded avenue after avenue in a period of a few years.

In a way, this disaster might have been a blessing in disguise. Suddenly, even the most insensitive lout on the town board of estimate could see how bare and ugly the roads and streets looked without trees to soften them. Many municipalities were shocked into forking over the money for planting, and as a result, many new street trees have been installed. Nowadays, even in large towns and big cities, squares have been cut out of the sidewalk and planted with trees, each one making a little green oasis in a large cement desert.

In garden-mad England, I noticed that every inch of space was planted with something; ferns grew on rooftops, violets grew on mossy walls, alpine sedum were set into cracks in the sidewalk. Was it beautiful? You bet. If you like to live in, among, by, and for gardens as I do, it was heaven.

Perhaps I'm obsessed, but I see gardens everywhere. I see airport runways and imagine what they would look like flanked by an allée of plane trees. I go down an escalator in a department store and imagine I'm gliding underneath philodendron-covered arches. I wait on line at my local post office and imagine beautiful dark red apples hanging over the heads of the postal employees. Sometimes I imagine plucking one of those beautiful vermillion apples and throwing it at one particular clerk who drives me crazy, or watching it fall with a satisfying kerplunk on top of his head.

So you can see that the idea of continuing the garden onto the grassy strip is hardly far-fetched, considering my mental condition.

3

USE PLANTS THAT GROW EASILY
IN YOUR CLIMATE AND LOCATION

I HAVE COME to this principle from bitter personal experience. My gardening friend Handsome Richard gave me a *Viburnum Carlesii,* also known as Korean spice bush, as a house gift about six years ago. I can honestly say that Richard is the best-looking friend I've ever had. If you think of Brad Pitt, you get an idea. When he came to my show once, the crew called him "Lady Chatterley's Lover," implying this manly beauty was my paramour. Nice fantasy.

Anyway, Richard gave me a *Viburnum Carlesii,* a shrub as good-looking as he. This type of viburnum has deep green leaves and, in late April and early May, waxy, pale pink-to-white flowers that win the divine fragrance award. The odor of viburnum flowers is as heavy, sweet, and voluptuous as a dream of love.

I planted it in the side garden several feet in front of a large lilac and next to a Chinese tree peony. The Chinese tree peony blooms in early May, at the same time as the lilac, and the flowers are eight to ten inches across and look as though they are made of pink crepe paper. When the lilac and tree peony bloom together, it's almost too much.

But not too much for me. I figured that the viburnum would add more, more, more pink and white sweetness to the sensual excess of this overblown horticultural experience, since it would bloom at the same time and add its subtle color and exquisite scent.

I think the fun of creating a garden is to make it as ravishing as possible. Why settle for nice and tasteful when you can have devastating? I want to make people swoon, or at least gasp with pleasure. Secretly I hoped that the combination of blooming lilac, viburnum, and Chinese tree peony would be beautiful enough to make the average person pass out cold.

Alas, it was not to be. I watered that little viburnum faithfully that first year, but it failed to thrive. It was three feet tall when I first planted it; the following spring it was two feet. Instead of an admirable dark green, its leaf color was sickly chartreuse. It developed a fungus. Bugs ate it. I did some research and learned that this viburnum prefers a woodsy, slightly acidic soil. My garden tends to be slightly alkaline because thirty years ago there used to be a cement plant in my town. So the lilac and the peony were very happy in my earth, but the viburnum was not.

That shrub meant a lot to me. Not only would it have added extra gloss to my garden the way a good red lipstick adds luster to my face, but it was a gift from an adorable friend who had moved away. Since I really loved this plant, I did the unthinkable: I went out and bought chemicals for it. I bought special food for acid-loving plants, the stuff that suburban homeowners pour on their puny evergreens when they turn yellow from the lime in the foundation cement. I lovingly applied it to the viburnum and, of course, it responded. Its healthy, dark green color returned and it even put out a few flowers the following spring. Since it did so well, I forgot about it, but the next year it languished again. Like a complaining relative, it reproached me constantly. I thought I could hear it coughing softly and whining to me whenever I passed. It lost leaves right in my face. I gave it more chemicals, which it devoured like an addict. Every time I forgot to give it a fix, it suffered, then rebounded unnaturally after a dose. Finally, I made the decision to pull the plug.

Last spring there was nothing left but a rotted stem, which I yanked out and threw on the compost. What did you expect, a requiem mass? It was a plant.

I loved that bush, but it hated my garden.

It was then I decided that the third principle of gardening should be to grow what grows easily in your yard. Think of the chemicals, the heartache, the money, the broken dreams that would have been saved if only I had followed this rule.

In place of the viburnum, I planted an Annabelle hydrangea (*Hydrangea arborescens* 'Annabelle'), which is now thriving. It's a charming bush, but to me, it's no *Viburnum Carlesii*. But then, not many shrubs are as good-looking as Handsome Richard.

WHERE TO PUT PLANTINGS IN RELATION TO THE HOUSE

Before you find what grows easily in your yard, it is helpful to know how much sunlight your garden gets each day, and when. As you may remember from schooldays, the rays of the sun are direct at the equator, but hit the rest of Earth at an angle, which changes depending on the season. In the summer, the sun's rays hit the northern hemisphere directly, hence the warm weather. In winter (vice versa), the sun is far to the south. It appears to rise in the southeast and set in the southwest. In northern places like Norway, Siberia, and Alaska, it never seems to rise at all in the winter, so noon and midnight are both dark.

While talking about gardening we find ourselves wandering into the realm of natural science. To little gardeners standing on our own tiny patch of Earth, what the planet does is of great significance because our fate is intimately tied to it. So is everyone else's, but nongardeners tend to ignore it on a day-to-day basis; they don't include it in their plans.

The angle of the sun as it moves across the sky is of great importance to gardeners. Excuse me, the angle of the sun as it *appears* to move across the sky is of great importance to us.

We need to plant in relation to the shadows cast by trees, buildings, hills. Since most of us have gardens adjacent to our house, we must take the sun's positions in relation to the building into account when we choose what plants to put in the garden.

Remember: The penalty for planting the wrong thing in the wrong place is death. The plant's.

Most suburban homes have land surrounding a freestanding house. In theory, that leaves the owner free to make the flower or vegetable garden anywhere he or she chooses. In practice, however, there are constraints. A sunny front yard seems to be the perfect place for a flower or vegetable garden, but most Americans are not comfortable spending a large amount of time in front, weeding this-end-up for all the neighbors to see. As I have mentioned ad nauseam, the only thing most people grow in the front yard is grass, and in many suburban towns it is illegal to have anything else.

My agent, Ken, lives on a fancy block in Scarsdale. He didn't get there on my 10 percent, believe me. He is an excellent gardener, but I'd love to see the expression on the neighbors' faces if my Ken tried to grow tomatoes in his front yard. Not to put too fine a point on it, it is considered low-class to grow cabbages, beans, or tomatoes and basil in the front yard in Scarsdale. Socially, it's worse than walking barefoot into a good restaurant, or wearing white shoes after Labor Day, or sleeping with the nanny. There are a lot of suburban neighborhoods like that.

Just to be perverse, last summer I grew a yellow plum tomato vine in my front yard. But I have a fence and a cottage-style garden out there, and I don't live in Scarsdale. In nonsuburban small towns, big cities, rural areas, and trailer parks, you do have a bit more social leeway to make any kind of garden you choose.

In neighborhoods where houses are close together, the side yards are too narrow for much planting or are taken up by utility areas such as garbage can storage or the driveway. The bedroom side of the house is almost aways useless, since it has no door and often overlooks the utility area of the neighbor's house. So most people have only one side of the house to make a really private, lovely garden, and that's in the back-yard. The direction in which this potential garden area faces is a matter of luck for most of us. (I've heard of Englishmen who will buy a house because "the garden has a lovely aspect," but I've never heard of an American who has done that.) The direction the area faces will determine what type of garden you can grow successfully.

EAST

The garden in my front yard faces east. By putting up the fence with a gate, I laid claim to the front yard so it was no longer a public space (see chapter 1). Naturally, I have filled this space with shrubs, flowers, and herbs, as well as the previously mentioned naughty—but I think rather sophisticated, even decadent—tomato vine.

The east-facing plants seem to be the happiest in the whole yard. They get at least half a day (six hours) of morning sun followed by a cool shady afternoon of peace and quiet. The plants think they're living in Oregon. Even sun worshipers like roses and dahlias love it, and it is healthier for everything else. There is less chance of fungal infections because the morning sun quickly dries the evening dew. From the point of view of the gardener, this exposure makes it possible to work in the garden in the afternoon shade without fainting from the heat.

If I had a choice, I would always choose an east-facing garden.

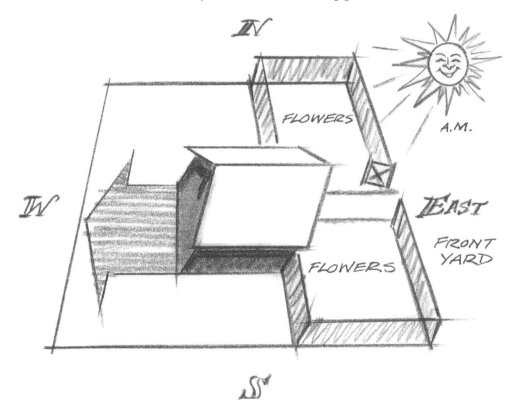

Gardening on the north-facing side of the house is the most difficult.

My friend Mary lives in a brownstone in Brooklyn. It has a little twenty-five-by-forty-foot garden in the back. It faces north, and wishing won't make it any different. Most of the garden is shaded by the brownstone, the rest is in dappled shade provided by surrounding trees.

Mary has a neighbor, Lettuce, who lives across the street. The garden behind Lettuce's brownstone faces south and Lettuce has planted it with a riot of flowering cottage garden perennials—roses, clematis vines, miniature cherry tree, spring bulbs—you get the idea.

In early spring, while Lettuce's garden is popping, Mary's is as cheerful as the back of her Frigidaire. While Lettuce breathes the fragrance of sun-warmed earth and sweet violets, Mary sits and waits, staring at muddy, icy clumps that look like undefrosted raw meat.

When she and her family first moved in, Mary said to me, "Cassandra, I'm in deep shade," although she didn't actually pronounce it that way.

I did my best to reassure her. On the plus side, a north-facing garden is cool in summer, a green oasis. Fewer weeds grow. Then again, so do fewer plants. And the colors of a north-facing garden are beautiful, if you like green.

"I like green now," my friend Mary says. "I've come to love it the way you come to love a stupid dog. It may not be the most desirable companion, but it's yours, and if you are faithful to it, it will be true to you." She has a stupid dog, so she ought to know.

What follows is an inspirational story, triumph in the face of adversity. Mary has had this garden for three years now, and she has been loyal to it. I think she has made a success of it.

The secret to success in a very shady garden is structure. When you have a limited number of plants that do well, they will be more interesting if framed by and contrasted with man-made objects. She has made a stone path leading from the doorway to a flagstone seating area. In addition to the garden plants, herbs are grown in groups of pots among one or two pieces of stone statuary, which look marvelous covered with moss. Needless to say, moss grows very well in Mary's garden.

After the first flush of spring bulbs and violets in May, the same ones that bloom in Lettuce's garden in April, the garden is basically green. In June, when Lettuce's garden is aflame with cascading roses, peonies, irises, etc., Mary's has one hybrid Exbury azalea with dark red blossoms. The name of the cultivar is unknown, since it was there when she moved in, but it is subtle and Oriental as it gracefully extends its branches, searching for light. The ground under the azalea is carpeted with pachysandra. Next to the azalea are lacy-leaved ferns. Next to the ferns are several varieties of hosta with large, dinner plate–size blue or light green or variegated leaves. These leaves are large and flat and a wonderful contrast to the delicate ferns. The best of this lot is a *Hosta plantaginea,* which I gave her from my garden. In August, it puts out large fragrant white bells—real flowers—that are much nicer than those dull, sickly lavender doo-dahs that pass for most hosta flowers.

Behind the azalea, dark blue–green ivy with maple-shaped leaves winds its way up the weathered-wood stockade fence. Opposite the azalea are more ferns and hostas, silver-and-green speckle-leafed pulmonaria, more ferns, a stone path, soft-blue Virginia bluebells (*Mertensia*), ferns. Under it all, *Lamium* 'White Nancy' creeps cheerfully onto the path and makes the ground appear sun-dappled, and Virginia creeper (*Parthenocissus quinquefolia*) winds its delicate tendrils around everything else.

In summer, Mary plants impatiens, that old warhorse of bleak city gardens. She uses only the pale pink- and white-flowered plants. In that way, she feels superior to Lettuce. "Her garden is overloaded with crass color and flowers," she observes. "Such a waste of all that sun."

There is more light at the back of the garden, since it is shaded only by the surrounding trees instead of the building. Here she has planted shade-tolerant flowering perennials, such as feathery pink astilbe, elegantly mauve hellebore, and snakeroot (*Cimicifuga racemosa*), whose flowers look like cream-colored fairy candles.

Behind the sitting area, blue and violet pansies in flower pots sit on the knee-high retaining wall, which is covered with Virginia creeper. There is one "sunny" corner (three hours per day in midsummer) that contains a blue-flowered lace-cap hydrangea (*Hydrangea macrophylla*), some columbines (*Aquilegia*), and handsome spires of self-sown foxgloves (*Digitalis purpurea*).

In front of the brick wall that separates her garden from the neighbor's yard, there is a pretty good juniper and a pretty pathetic holly. She wants to take the holly out altogether, but I've convinced her not to, because I think it will come back and because I like holly. Next to the holly is an ancient privet, the lone survivor of what must have been a hedge around 1923. Mary says, "I've been wrestling with my conscience about what to do with it. Right now it is a stump with branches spouting out of it like hairs from a wart." Should she keep it small, let it grow tall, make it into a topiary lightbulb, or take it out? Time will tell.

Behind the juniper, she keeps the secret of her garden's success: the compost heap.

When you have very little sun, it's essential to keep the soil in excellent condition. It makes all the difference between having a garden that thrives even in full shade and a murky wasteland worthy of T. S. Eliot. Shade plants love a soil that is rich in organic material. In nature, they would be growing on the floor of the woodland, which is full of humus and leaf mold. Mary doesn't use chemical fertilizers because she is an organic gardener, and since plants grow slowly in low light, they have no use for extra chemicals anyway. They do much better with the kitchen-scrap compost that Mary gives them.

Every spring, she applies a wood chip mulch, which not only adds more organic material to the soil but makes it unnecessary to water except during periods of drought.

All over the place, Mary has big clumps of the most robust and reliable denizen of this garden, old-fashioned spiderwort (*Tradescantia virginiana*), which is a lot better-looking than its common name would suggest. Its "intense" lavender-blue flowers bloom for a long time in summer. (*Intense* is a catalog term. It's dark lavender-blue.) She has a lot of spiderwort—in fact, it fills every spare nook. It was growing there when she first started to make the garden, and I have no doubt it will be there long after she moves out. "Why fight it?" I observed when I first saw the stuff. "You might as well grow a lot of it, because nothing else seems to like this place as much."

She agreed, mainly to avoid a fight, with me or with the spiderwort, which will fight back harder than I do. It has turned out wonderfully. Having a lot of one particular plant gives the garden individuality. Anyone visiting in summer would describe Mary as "the gardener with all those spiderworts!" I know, I know, it sounds repulsive, but trust me, with the pink and white impatiens, the astilbe, the white-flowered hostas, and the creamy candles of the snakeroot, it looks really nice.

Like all gardens that are tended with a feeling for the special qualities of a specific place, Mary's garden has unique personality and style. There is something elegant about sitting on a designer garden chair in Mary's cool green garden with nothing but pink, blue, and cream-colored blossoms all around you, the only touch of bright color the ruby red of the very good Bordeaux in your crystal goblet, as you make witty remarks to your admiring friends.

WEST

The west side of the house is another story, and I don't mean a musical by Leonard Bernstein. This west-side story is about heat, sun blazing as hot as Chita Rivera's cha-cha-cha. By three o'clock on a July afternoon in a west-facing garden, plants are wilting and the gardener is sleeping.

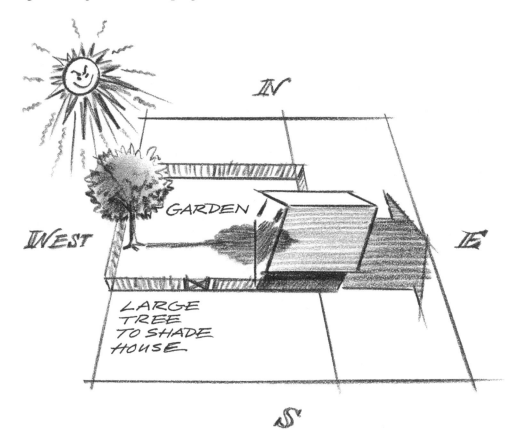

The best way to handle a large west-facing garden is to plant something tall at the west end, thereby shading the garden from the hottest part of the day, so you can work in comfort in the afternoon. Of course, if the garden is small, and the west side of the house is the only place you have to grow your vegetables, you have no choice but to do your weeding and watering in the morning and go indoors and take a nap in the afternoon, which isn't such a bad idea, come to think of it.

If I had somewhere else to put my flower or vegetable garden, I would forget the flowers and plant deciduous trees on the west side of the house to provide shade in summer, thereby lowering the temperature inside and saving air-conditioning costs. When the tree leaves have fallen in winter, the sun can warm the house all afternoon. In hot climates, shading the west side of the house is such an obvious advantage that I'm shocked to see that it is not universally done in the southern part of the country, especially in the Southwest.

As I mentioned in the first chapter, traditionally the west side of the house is the place to erect a pergola, a porch, a loggia, or other type of overhanging roof, which keeps the sun out of the house all afternoon and provides dappled shade at all times of the year.

With the advent of air-conditioning, porches, loggias, and even window awnings have fallen into disuse. Who needs to keep the sun out when you have a machine to keep everything cool? Only lately are we seeing a return to these low-tech, energy-saving, absolutely lovely methods of climate modification.

On the plus side, a west-facing garden provides a good half-day of sun during most of the year and a full eight hours in summer when the days are longest, a treat for many plants.

It also has lovely sunsets.

SOUTH

If I were growing vegetables, I would make my garden on the south side of the house. Ah love the South, y'all, because the Southland gets sun all the live-long day. That sounds like a Stephen Foster song, doesn't it? A south-facing garden may be perfect for growing a bale of cotton, but perhaps not so fabulous for an idyllic garden in which to dwell on a hot summer afternoon.

For noncommercial gardeners, it is not desirable to have large uninterrupted areas of relentless, hatless, sun-baked earth. A south-facing aspect gives you the opportunity to design the garden with sunny areas as well as with structures that provide shade, like arbors and gazebos, trees, and large shrubs. In a small south-facing garden, it is a good

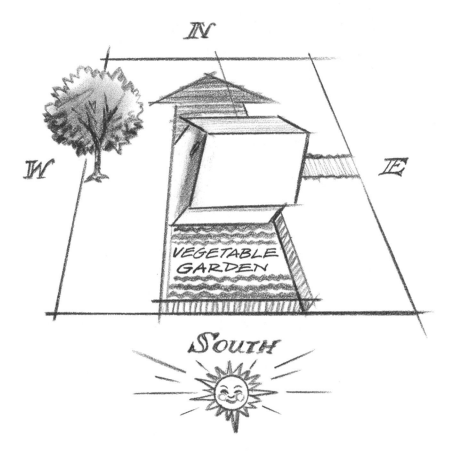

idea to plant trees on the west side for the same reason you plant trees on the west side of a house—it will keep everything from baking, fading, and wilting in the afternoon sun, especially the gardener.

Mary's neighbor Lettuce has a lovely old cherry tree on the west side of her south-facing garden, bless her. Not only does it provide a spring cherry blossom display worthy of the second act of *Madame Butterfly* and give gentle, dappled shade to the gorgeous riot of flowering perennials underneath, it also makes the small garden a cooler place to sit on a hot summer afternoon. Not as cool as Mary's yard, though. Ha-ha.

Not all gardens face perfectly north, east, south, or west, of course. Like people, they are usually a little off, but that's okay.

My flower garden off the side porch faces southeast, a most pleasant aspect. The sun peeks over the top of the front lilac bush in the morning, and by afternoon it disappears behind the vegetable patch next to the garage. Feel free to envy me, but I didn't plan it that way, I swear. Like most people, all I wanted to do was to put the garden where I could get a little privacy and create a nice view from my most frequent vantage point, the side porch near the kitchen. But when I realized that the area happened to face southeast, I was glad—*glad,* I tell you!

To be honest, I'm not sure the location of my garden was by chance. No, I'm not implying any religious-type experience. No angel came down and blessed me, horticulturally speaking, for having been good in a former life, or anything like that. The real reason was more mundane, but also more interesting.

My house was built in the nineteenth century using the low-tech methods for climate control in the pre-air-conditioned, pre–centrally heated world. In those days, architects would situate the house so that the parlor faced north or northeast. This kept the front rooms cool in the summer and prevented the sun from shining into the house and fading the velvet draperies and upholstered furniture of the "best" room. The kitchen, home of the servants, was placed at the rear of the house, farthest from the parlor, usually on the south or southwest side, which made the kitchen hot. But the kitchen windows in my old house have been placed for maximum coolness. There is one facing north, and another facing south, which is shaded by the side porch to keep it as cool as possible. In winter, the room was kept warm by the wood-burning stove.

Houses have been built to adjust for climate this way throughout history, even in America, as I have noted when talking about the Creole courtyards of New Orleans. Since the 1960s, however, everyone I know has built big south-facing double doors that lead out to an uncovered deck. Sun, sun flooding the house! You could get a beautiful Florida suntan even indoors! It was so fashionable, who would have guessed how bad it was for you?

Now, at the beginning of the twenty-first century, we've finally come to realize the wisdom of our forefathers when it came to building for your climate, and to keeping your head out of the sun.

Adapting to the Sun, the Old-Fashioned Way

The design of ancient buildings in arid regions of the world is a perfect example of the way architecture and garden design can be adapted to nature, and by so doing create a style of distinctive and harmonious beauty. Take the houses and gardens of ancient Persia, for example.

Over thousands of years, the Persians developed ways of coping with heat, and these building designs are still in use. (But Western influence has taken its toll. Modern "upscale" buildings in Iran are boring replicas of the same, air-conditioned shoe boxes you see all over the world from Toronto to Timbuktu, Moscow to Manila.)

In the desert, whole cities are designed for climate modification. Main streets are narrow and run north-south so that pedestrians are shaded from both the morning (eastern) and afternoon (western) sun. Sometimes arches span the streets, sheltering the merchants of the bazaar who transact business in alcoves underneath. When residential streets intersect the north-south thoroughfare, the arches create a vaulted area, a great room called a *timcah*. A *timcah* will often be devoted to one type of merchandise or craftsmen's guild. For example, one area will be for fabric stalls, another one for spices, etc.

A Persian bazaar resembles a suburban shopping mall, right down to the coffee bars. It is the perfect way to display goods, and a convenient way to shop for them. Many older American towns are beginning to adopt this bazaar idea as well by restricting automobile traffic on city streets, making them into pedestrian malls.

Located at right angles to the main street, the side streets of the old cities are where the private houses are located. Entire residential neighborhoods are often enclosed by walls and can be entered only by arched gateways, a practice that is presently being emulated in wealthy communities in the United States.

The private houses are designed for maximum coolness. The walls are thick and the roofs are vaulted to trap hot air in high ceilings. There are structures on the roofs that look like chimneys, with openings on the side. These are wind towers. The openings are turned to the prevailing wind, which whistles down this reverse chimney to cool the interior of the house.

There are no windows at all on the west side of the house for reasons previously mentioned. In Iran, the temperature in the afternoon sun might reach 120 degrees.

Private homes are built around an interior courtyard. In the desert, these courtyards are set several feet below ground level to shade as much surface as possible during the day. There is a social as well as a climatic reason for this. The interior courtyard garden is the domain of the women. Keeping them partly underground is a good way to make sure they are unseen, hidden, and inaccessible to the outside world. They are oppressed, but less so by the heat than they otherwise are.*

This house arrangement causes a profound difference in the way the garden is perceived. To us, the house is the place, the garden is the decorative surrounding area. To them, the garden is the central room of the house.

In our secular, liberated country, the purpose of an interior garden would be similar to that in Persia, but not the same. (Thank heavens!) A home is no longer the domain, chief occupation, and prison of female existence. The purpose here would be to make a naturally cool, private place in the midst of a hectic, noisy, stressful, demanding, modern environment that puts us all on sensory overload. Wouldn't it be nice to have our own private outdoor paradise away from highways, truck routes, boom boxes, door-to-door salesmen, neighbors with guns, drunks, ex-husbands, in-laws, bill collectors, religious fanatics, and other people's children, to name just a few? We get the word *paradise* from the Persian language. It means "a garden."

We can learn a lot from the way other cultures adapted to their environments long before there was electricity or modern appliances, especially since we Americans seem to like hot climates. Americans flock to places like Florida and Southern California, and most people tell me it's because they love the weather. My aunt Pauline lives in Boca Raton—"for the climate," she says. In fact, she needs air-conditioning ten months of the year, otherwise she would faint, I mean literally pass out on the floor. I know that if her condominium had hot weather–designed architecture instead of barracks-as-stucco condos, she would only need air-conditioning for eight months a year, and with a small enclosed courtyard garden, might even get to enjoy the natural climate once in a while.

Design for Arid Regions, ed. Gideon S. Golany (New York: Van Nostrand Reinhold Co., 1983).

My Path to Happiness

I began this chapter by talking about growing plants that are well adapted to the environment and wound up by talking about houses, gardens, even whole cities that are adapted to the environment. To the extent that we put ourselves in accord with Mother Nature, our physical life becomes easier, less wasteful, and more productive, and it follows as the night does the day that our mental lives will improve as well. Believe me, I'm not trying to make any earthshaking claims here. This is no self-help manual disguised as a humorous gardening book, and I'm no Deepak Chopra. All I can say is, if you make a garden in harmony with the environment, you will have joy, sensuous delight, physical beauty, personal virtue, eternal wisdom, and the peace that passeth understanding.

Before going any further in this chapter about plants that are easy to grow, I feel I must include a list of plants that the deer and other herbivore wildlife won't eat. This is by popular request. Everywhere I go to speak, across the length and breadth of the country, from San Francisco to Florida to Vermont, the most common problem among gardeners is what to do about the deer. If you live in an area that is infested with the darlings—and who doesn't?—the one qualifying attribute for an easily grown plant is that it is unappetizing for animals to eat. Even though it may be perfectly suited to its soil and climate, no plant will grow easily if it keeps getting its leaves gobbled. So, while most of us wouldn't want to have a garden made up *only* of plants that deer won't eat, it's nice to have a few for insurance.

If you have already wisely fenced off the yard so that deer are no longer a problem inside the garden, the plants listed here are useful for areas outside the enclosure.

This list is by no means all-inclusive, but for the desperate, I can assure you that deer dislike these plants intensely. Look, I don't want to get any letters from people who say that deer ate their specimen of one of these plants. Of course, an absolutely starving deer will eat anything. A word of caution: Many of these plants are poisonous. It's too bad we can't get the deer to eat them! (Be aware that they are poisonous to humans and domestic animals as well.)

PLANTS THAT THE DEER WON'T EAT (MOST OF THE TIME)

To find deer-resistant plants, in general look for these qualities:

- **Very aromatic leaves**
- **Gray leaves**
- **Hairy, fuzzy, or painfully spiny leaves**

Monkshood, wolfbane (*Aconitum*)
A member of the buttercup or Ranunculus family, all of which are poisonous. Ranunculus is one of the oldest intact plant families on earth. That's because not many animals eat members of the buttercup family twice.

Yarrow (*Achillea*)
Especially the gray-leaved variety called Moonbeam.

Chives and ornamental onions (*Allium*)
These bloom at the same time as tulips, but unlike tulips are revolting to deer.

Pearly everlasting (*Anaphalis*)
It is gray, hairy, and sticky.

Anchusa
My friend Peter quotes an old farmer's poem: "Always refuse a gift of *Anchusa*." Not exactly Keats, eh? *Anchusa* is supposed to seed itself all over the place, although it never does in my garden. So much for old farmer's poems. I love it. The leaves of this plant have a fuzz that looks like hair on a pig's back, but the plant also has bright, true blue flowers, a rare and precious color in the garden.

Columbine (*Aquilegia*)
Also a member of the poisonous Ranunculus family. The light airy flowers look beautiful with allium, and bloom at the same time.

Anemone
All anemones are members of the notorious Ranunculus clan, including Japanese anemone (*Anemone japonica*), windflower (*Anemone blanda*), florist's anemone (*Anemone coronaria*), and the Pasque flower (*Anemone pulsatilla*).

Wormwood (*Artemesia*)
It's gray and it smells.

Aromatic Herbs
Sage, catnip, thyme, oregano, etc. Remember, the stronger the odor, the better.

Snakeroot (*Cimicifuga*)
This is a stately, shade-loving plant that should be grown in every garden anyway. It's also a Ranunculus.

Clematis: all varieties
Why don't deer like these gorgeous plants? They are all Ranunculus, and we can thank our lucky stars.

Bleeding heart (*Dicentra spectabilis* and *Dicentra eximia*)
Great shade plants.

(continued on next page)

Foxglove (*Digitalis*)
It's poisonous.

Globe thistle (*Echinops*)
And look for other thistles, like Scotch thistle (*Onopordum acanthium*). Also sea holly and Miss Wilmott's Ghost, both forms of *Eryngium*, a beautiful but cruel-looking group of plants. I'll bet they taste like the "choke" of an artichoke.

Cranesbill, geraniums (*Geranium spp.*)
This is the perennial of temperate gardens. It makes mounds of pink, blue, or white flowers for the edge of the border or as a ground cover. I grow several varieties, none of which get eaten.

Iris: all varieties
The Siberian irises are especially easy to grow.

Sea lavender (*Limonium*)
Also know as statice. It's dry and has somewhat hairy, unappetizing leaves.

Bee balm (*Monarda*)
Colorful, quickly spreading perennial whose leaves and flowers smell to me like some kind of pickle/tea combination. Mediciney.

Daffodil (*Narcissus*)
All varieties are poisonous. A good way to fool browsing animals is to plant daffodils around or in the same hole, as you plant lilies and other vulnerable bulbs. A deer nuzzling the ground for edible bulb shoots will turn away from the daffodil leaves and not notice the emerging lilies or tulips nearby. Ha-ha.

Evening primrose (*Oenothera missouriensis*)
Another Ranunculus. I've never seen anything eat its close relative, sundrops (*Oenothera fruticosa*), either.

Peony (*Paeonia*)
A Ranunculus, and a queen of the clan.

Oriental poppy (*Papaver orientale*)
It has hairy leaves. But in my experience, other poppies like Iceland poppy (*P. naudicaule*), the annual California poppy (*P. californicum*), and the opium poppy (*P. somniferum*) don't get eaten either.

Globeflower (*Trollius*)
Woodland shade lover that has elegant, usually yellow flowers and a Ranunculus pedigree.

Meadow rue (*Thalictrum*)
A Ranunculus. There are several garden-worthy species of meadow rue—the three-foot *Thalictrum aquilegiafolium*, with flowers that resemble pink-feather down, and *Thalictrum Delavayi*, with lavender or white flowers. Try them all. They love moist semishade.

Roast beef, lamb, chicken, venison
If you can find a plant that is made of meat, deer will definitely not eat it.

Rose-of-Sharon (*Hibiscus syriacus*)
I love this late-summer shrub with hibiscus flowers.

Potentilla (*Potentilla fruticosa*)
This two- to five-foot shrub is great for all kinds of difficult conditions. Flowers resemble yellow, white, or pink strawberry blossoms.

Spruce (*Picea*)
I know it's a tree, but there are dwarf varieties.

Russian sage (*Perovskia atriplicifolia*)
Has blue flowers on gray leaves, blooms in summer, and tastes like soap. What more could you ask?

Holly (*Ilex*)
Okay, deer will nosh an occasional leaf, but they spit it out.

Bridal wreath spirea (*Spiraea Vanhouttei*)
I have several varieties of spirea besides this one in my garden and none of them get eaten. A good bet.

I have confined this list to those plants that I know from firsthand experience are deer-resistant. The list is by no means exhaustive, but I would rather err on the side of caution. Recently, I read a "deer-resistant" plant list in a catalog and it included hosta, yew, daylilies, and other deer treats. Deer like nothing better than the juicy leaves of hosta and the succulent buds of daylilies, just before they open. What a cruel joke on anyone who followed that list!

HOW TO FIND THE BEST PLANTS FOR YOUR GARDEN

The most entertaining way to find out what grows best in your particular garden is by the process of elimination. Most of us have used this method, although usually not on purpose. All it requires is that you go the nursery and buy every perennial in sight. Go hog-wild. It's expensive, but boy, is it fun.

Now go home and plant. After a season or two, it will be dramatically obvious which varieties prefer your garden and vice versa. Some plants will have died outright, some will have done so-so, and some will have threatened to overwhelm the whole place. The lustiest and most lovable survivors, barring those that threaten to take over, will be the basis for your seasonal designs.

There are several cheaper ways to find out which plants are easy to grow in your area. First, find out by reading garden books. "But *which* garden books?" you well may ask.

American vs. British Garden Books

For the better part of this century, Americans have gotten their gardening advice from English writers, and we owe a tremendous debt to them. As a result of their influence, however, our plant choices have been heavily biased in favor of plants that do well in the British Isles. The trouble is that England is a plant paradise compared to most of North America. It rains every day there and the temperature rarely rises into the nineties in summer. When it turned hot and dry in the summer of 1990, the British were shocked, and it's not as easy to shock the British as it used to be since they produced the Rolling Stones. During the 1980s, they have been very concerned with water shortages and heat.

Winters are mild. In most of the British Isles, frost is considered dangerous and they are excited by snow. Although Great Britain is much farther north than the United States—most of it is on the same northern latitude as Canada—its climate is influenced by the Gulf Stream, a warm current that comes up from the South Atlantic and delivers a steam bath of foggy weather and moderate winters. Without the Gulf Stream, the weather in London would resemble the weather in Nova Scotia.

It makes me happy that the British can grow practically any plant in the world, including the *Meconopsis,* the Himalayan blue poppy, a flower so rare, so beautiful, so true blue, that a nineteenth-century English botanist committed murder to obtain one specimen. I just made that up, but I bet there probably were crazy botanists like that in England.

With the exception of the Pacific Northwest, as already mentioned, most of North America has hotter summers and/or colder winters than England and very few parts of the North American continent get as much consistent rain. In New England, the Rockies, and other mountainous places, summers are cool, winters are very, very cold. In the South, winters are warm, summers are very, very hot.

Yet for years, American gardeners have landscaped like Englishmen. We still do. We have gone to great lengths to make our homes resemble a greensward-covered English landscape. All right, I don't want to belabor the point about lawns. I'm afraid I've flogged that mare to death. (Note: That was only a metaphor. No animals were harmed in the writing of this book.)

The fragrant herb lavender is the sort of fantasy plant that we are always trying to grow in this country. All the English garden books rave over it, and it does grow wonderfully well in England, but not in my neighborhood. In my area, it will live through two winters and get killed by a third, just when it's starting to look good. So instead of struggling with lavender, I prefer catnip (*Nepeta Mussinii*), which grows like crazy in my American garden.

A friend of mine, Jackie O. (not that one), planted a border of twenty varieties of yellow roses and wanted to use lavender as an underplanting. I thought it was a beautiful idea in theory. Yellow with soft lavender blue is a classic combination.

"Forget it, Jackie O.," I told her. "Plant catnip." I went on to explain that catnip looks very similar to lavender and will thrive and form a wonderful ground cover under the roses. She objected that catnip wasn't the traditional plant to use with roses, and doesn't catnip attract cats?

"You've been reading too many English gardening books," I told her, and explained that, unlike lavender, catnip wouldn't die every other winter and have to be replaced; on the contrary, it will increase and can be divided so that there will be enough to completely cover the ground under the roses practically for free. And yes, it does attract cats. What's wrong with cats?

Convinced by the logic of my arguments and a fondness for felines, she decided to do it. But before she had a chance to put the idea into practice, she got a divorce instead. (I saw a similar combination at another friend's house, and it looked marvelous.) Incidently, chives also look good and don't attract cats.

The gardening book situation has changed quite a bit in the past few years. Now there are hundreds of wonderful gardening books (too many) by Americans, whose experiences and plant choices are appropriate to our conditions. Read them.

Ken Druse celebrates native American plants. Allen Lacy's *The Garden in Autumn* is all about the magic of that season, which is much more thrilling in North America than it is in England, with our crisp frosts and gorgeous leaf colors. Linda Yang's *The City and Town Gardener* is for urban areas. Pamela Jones tells all about *Just Weeds*.

There are books that specialize in plants for your part of the country, or that focus on your particular problem. *Water-wise Gardening*, by Thomas Christopher, is all about succeeding in dry regions. Books with specific titles, like *Herbs for Southern Gardens* or *Native Trees of the Northwest* may never make the *New York Times* bestseller list, but they are available in the gardening section. Some titles are even more specialized, like *Wildflowers of Southern Ontario Roadsides; Landscaping Your Central Florida Trailer Park; Know and Grow Edible Pods of Flushing, Queens; Very, Very Small Ferns of Virginia,* etc. I made those titles up, but books like these exist in local bookstores and can be found in the libraries of agricultural colleges and local botanical gardens. As a member of the Horticultural Society of New York, I have the privilege of using their incredible library, starring that indefatigable librarian Katherine Powis, the queen of horticultural knowledge.

Garden Catalogs

Many gardeners I know get a lot of their information from garden catalogs. It's true that you can learn a lot about plants from good garden catalogs. It's also true that you can learn nothing except a lot of cheesy marketing practices from bad garden catalogs. I have received my share of both kinds over the years, and there are a few elements to look out for. A good catalog tells you a plant's botanical name, hardiness zone, eventual height, bloom time, whether it prefers sun or shade, especially acid or alkaline conditions, or other bits of information pertinent to its culture and growing habits. A *very* good catalog will tell you the truth. It will indicate if the plant is a thug or if it is temperamental, under what conditions it will succeed, and when to avoid planting it.

Understandably, no company is going to tell you outright that its product is lousy, but the catalog should give enough information to let you decide if it is useful to you. To its credit, the Thompson and Morgan catalog will aways tell you if a particular seed is easy, so-so, or difficult to germinate.

Here's a description of a Fortune's holly fern from a very good catalog, Carroll Gardens, 444 East Main Street, Westminster, MD 21157:

> (Fern) Holly, Fortune's *Cyrtomium fortunei*
> Zone 6 (with protection)–10
> Fronds of shiny, leathery, deep green (resembling Oregon grape holly) arch ever so slightly as they arise from large, scaly rhizomes to form open, vase-shaped, 12–18" clumps. Fortune's holly fern, the hardiest of the Oriental holly ferns, is distinguished by its narrow, upright fronds with smooth-edged leaflets. Choose a heavily shaded, slightly moist, very well drained site. Woodsy soil, amended with limestone chips, is best. Protection from winter wind is important, especially in zones 6 and 7. 3 for $16.85

I can almost hear the rustle of the deep green leaves and smell that woodsy-mossy aroma. If I am going to drop seventeen bucks (not including postage and handling) for three little specimens of these ferns, I appreciate knowing that, unlike most woodsy ferns, this variety likes lime. And I also appreciate their accurate description of the hardiness of this variety. Of course, I won't buy this fern, because my area is too cold, but Carroll Gardens's honesty has won my admiration, and although a sale was lost, they have won my heart and my business.

The catalog from Plant Delights Nursery, Inc., at Juniper Level Botanic Gardens, 9241 Sauls Road, Raleigh, NC 27603, is complete and fun to read. It is written in the first person by the president of the company, Tony Avent:

> Yucca thompsoniana (Thompson's Yucca) $6.00
> Sun, Zone 4–10, 24". Origin USA
> This is one of my favorite tree yuccas. The single trunk, covered with dried leaves, blue-gray foliage and a single head, makes for a spectacular specimen . . . most closely resembles boxing promoter Don King's hairdo on a tall fence post. In late spring, the plants are topped with 4' spike of white bell-like flowers. Catalog #01767

It is one of the few times reading a catalog has made me laugh.

Some catalogs are funny, but not on purpose. Here's one from a catalog that shall remain nameless, because I don't want to hear from the company's lawyers. We have seen similar tabloid-type catalogs, with descriptions that scale to new heights of horticultural hyperbole! The author of this one must have started his career writing ad copy for the circus.

NEW JUMBO EVERBLOOMING DAHLIAS!

Dahlia Summer Bliss!

This everblooming raspberry-red beauty actually starts blooming two weeks before others! The flowers are larger and the number of flowers are superior! Moreover, the autumn flower production is phenomenal! New Summer Bliss! changes the blooming season from a trickle to an avalanche!—big!, round!, red! flowers begin to open in early summer, but reach a crescendo! during autumn months when big! blooms from the garden are scarce! We ship gorgeous! tubers for big! red! blooms the first season! Summer Bliss! Dahlia!: 6 tubers $9.98

The problem with this kind of description is that, as a source of horticultural information, it stinks. After reading this entry, I don't know any more about dahlias than I would if I just fell out of a jumbo dahlia tree. Nowhere, here or elsewhere in the catalog, does it tell you anything about these plants except that they are big (!), red (!), and come as gorgeous (!) tubers. No mention of hardiness zone, so we're left to assume it's hardy everywhere. Have you ever seen a dahlia tuber? *Gorgeous* is not a word I would use to describe it. "A fat ugly yam," is more like it. I don't buy from catalogs like this one. Although that red dahlia *does* sound tempting.

Most garden catalogs are designed to sell to the widest possible audience, and it is hard to find one suitable for your particular area unless the company is in your town. I prefer to order from nurseries that are located in a part of the country with a climate similar to mine. After losing a couple of shrubs that I had bought from a company in Florida, I became suspicious of garden catalogs from the Deep South. Perhaps these plants weren't as hardy as the author of the catalog descriptions would have me believe. Perhaps the catalog author believed himself, but what did he know? He was sitting in Tampa among the camellias, sipping a mint julip and nibbling pecans.

Sometimes garden catalogs offer collections. This is an economical way to get a lot of plants at once. Most of the time the collections feature specialty items. For example, Shepherd's Seeds features collections of herbs, herbal teas, edible flowers, flowering vines, hummingbird flowers, and sunflowers, just to name a few. Inevitably, some of the varieties will do better in your garden than others, and this is a good way to sample a wide variety and find out which ones are best for you. Bluestone Perennials, 7211 Middle Ridge Road, Madison, OH 44057, offers a "Perennial Starter Garden," which includes a selection of flowering plants as well as a planting map for a sixteen-by-four-foot area. (I would have made it sixteen by nine, using Greek classical proportion.)

I wish some garden catalog would offer collections that address particular gardening problems, like "Plants for Damp, Shady Places," "A Dry, Hot Garden," "The Untalented Gardener's Collection for Sun." Some try, but they could be more specific. It would be an excellent marketing ploy.

Garden Centers, Landscapers

If you are blessed with a really good garden center in your area, it can be almost as useful as a horticultural library. A garden center that has been in business for a while has had its share of returns and failures, and chances are they won't stock a loser plant. (All right, yes they will, if it's popular enough.) For the most part, however, a good garden center offers plants that will thrive locally, and they offer them at the right time for planting. Good local garden centers in Arizona will have very different inventories than those in Vermont. Bad garden centers have the same plants everywhere in the country.

I hesitate to recommend that you consult a professional landscaper to find good locally adapted plants, because so few of the commercial companies are horticulturally sophisticated. Landscapers on Long Island offer five shrubs and fifty million pieces of sod, which they will place in any and all situations. So they are worse than no help at all. However, this is changing slowly. Here and there, you can find landscaping companies that feature well adapted plant materials calling for low-maintenance and low-chemical gardening practices. Sometimes they will state this in their newspaper ad:

"We do natural, environmentally friendly landscaping," or words to that effect. (I'd settle for "friendly landscaping.") It might be worthwhile to give them a call.

The Thrifty Way to Get Good Ideas

It pays to look for plants that do well in areas with a climate similar to yours. Plants of the Mediterranean do well in the American Southwest, so a variety that thrives in Greece would do well in Fresno, California; the climate of Seattle is similar to the British Isles; Minnesota is similar to the Ukraine. If you study up on the flora of these exotic places, it's easy to find unusual plants that will do well in your particular climate, and the exotic locale may provide you with inspiration, not to mention a possible destination for your next vacation. You can go there to observe the flowers.

Observation of local yards is helpful. What grows well in the neighborhood? Grow a lot of that. Don't worry that it will be boring; a lot of anything looks good if you like it, even forsythia. Oh, yes. It looks a lot better than grass. And if your neighbor is snotty about it and says, "Oh, everyone has one of those," you can say, "Yes, but I have more!"

Visit the countryside with the same attention that you would give to the shoes in Thom McAn's if you were barefoot. The garden needs plants the way you need footwear. Shop the countryside for plants that take care of themselves without a gardener. What plants are most beautiful? When do they bloom? Do they come in size seven and a half? Note whether they are growing on a mountaintop, in the boggy ditch along the roadside, in the shade of trees, or next to a limestone outcropping. A plant that does well next to a limestone rock will also be happy near a cement foundation, which is full of lime. Yes, you may get stuck with a number of weeds this way, but you will find a number of treasures as well.

Before I go any further, I must say that I am against digging up plants in the wild. I do not go to Yosemite National Park or any other designated wild place to find plants. It's illegal. I know I have been accused of advocating theft to obtain plant specimens. Just because I said, "If you take a division of a perennial in the middle of the night, hardly anyone will ever notice," I didn't mean that you should run out and do it! If I told you to jump off the Brooklyn Bridge, would you do it? There is no law against keeping a shovel in the trunk of your car, however. One should steal plants only as a last resort, and only from mean people who are about to mow them down.

I needn't tell you that the greatest danger to wildflowers is not from gardeners. A legion of gardeners could take divisions all day and never do the damage of one shopping center parking lot. I consider any plant growing in the vicinity of a parking lot a pagan baby waiting for me to save it from eternal perdition.

One such plant was joe-pye weed (*Eupatorium purpureum*), which I found growing along the drainage ditch of a parking lot. It is one of my favorite plants of the countryside. According to garden writer Allen Lacy, the name "joe pye" refers either to a medicine man who cured typhoid fever with a tea brewed from the leaves, or the Native American word *jopi,* which means typhoid.*

The fact that the name of the plant comes from a deadly disease makes it sound repulsive, but trust me, this is a gorgeous, well-behaved plant. It has clumps of tall, wiry stems that support large, dusty-pink, cloud-like umbrellas composed of hundreds of tiny florets. It's not magenta, I swear. Along the roadside, it grows from three to six feet high, but will get taller under cultivation. It reaches ten feet tall in Allen Lacy's garden. Mine grows to about five or six feet, but my clump is only two years old and not so well established. The parking lot where I found the joe-pye weed surrounded a small strip mall of perhaps five stores near Rhineville, New York. This is a beautiful town, but it really should get some zoning laws. Once these ugly little mall-ettes get going, a charming town can quickly turn into a sprawling Nowheresville, U.S.A., with endless roadways leading to the thruway and its town center a deserted husk. This mall-ette had been erected in an area that had previously been a lovely sloping meadow near a woodland.

Horticultural treasures grew around that parking lot, the survivors of the blacktop massacre. In addition to the joe-pye weed, I counted seven different varieties of asters, including the tall lavender-blue New England aster (*Aster novae-angliae*), soft white-pink sprays of *Aster cordifolius* and *Aster pilosus*. There were also several different vari-

---

*Allen Lacy, *The Garden in Autumn* (New York: Atlantic Monthly Press, 1990).

eties of goldenrod (*Solidago*), black-eyed susans (*Rudbeckia hirta*), and dame's rocket (*Hesperis matronalis*).

Neglecting to take my own advice, I had no shovel in the car, not even a trowel. I had to use the windshield scraper, and a messy job it was, too. I managed to dig up a small piece of joe-pye root along with a few leaves, however, and I was in business. You don't need to take the whole plant; that I would never do, even to save a specimen from the bulldozer. Well, maybe then. I planted it in my side garden, planning for it to bloom next to a rose-of-Sharon bush, which also has mauve flowers, although in a somewhat brighter shade of pink. Between the rose-of-Sharon and the joe-pye weed were a dozen self-sown airy spots of *Verbena bonariensis,* which look like purple-pink buttons on five-foot wires, along with self-sown *Nicotiana alata,* the fragrant white progenitor of the pink-and-red Nikki Mix flowering tobacco you see on sale at garden centers in the spring.

The joe-pye weed looked pretty pathetic when I first planted it. Its one stem, the victim of a collision with the windshield scraper, listed drunkenly. I piled up dirt on the opposite side of the stem to nudge it erect, but no go. I tried talking dirty to it. Plants love dirt, but as soon as I walked away, it fell over again. After a couple of attempts, I left it. The poor, mangled bit of root was lucky to be alive.

That was last summer. This year, it grew straight to about five feet and even managed to put out a few more stems. It had one mauve umbel, and I'm looking forward to more in the years to come.

A DESERT GARDEN

To get an idea of what a garden of well-adapted plants might look like, let me give you a dramatic example.

Say we have a garden near Tucson, Arizona. The climate is so drastic, it forces us to make special allowances for it. First, there is the desert sun, relentless as a Jewish mother. To modify its effects, we erect six-foot adobe walls around three sides of the area we wish to cultivate, protecting the garden from drying desert winds and providing shade near its base for at least some part of every day. The house itself constitutes the fourth wall.

Instead of making raised beds, the way we might do in the Northeast, we make sunken beds, so that all the rainwater that falls is directed right to the roots of our plantings. We use plenty of stones in a dry garden, not only because they look good and retain moisture, but also because plants love to snuggle up to stones to keep their feet damp.

In one corner of the garden, we plant agave. Its name in Greek means illustrious or noble. And it is! Some varieties are huge, but we plant *Agave tequilana*, the one they use to make the famous booze, although I myself would never use it for that purpose, any more than I would make dope out of my pretty opium poppies (*Papaver somniferum*). This one has two-and-a-half-foot, three-inch-wide bluish-gray leaves that are architectural as heck, and sprouts a fifteen-foot flower stalk when in bloom. I balance this with some bear grass (*Yucca glauca*) on the other side of the garden. It has three-foot-long bluish leaves with lots of curly threads among them. It also has spikes of tall, pale, bell-shaped flowers.

The local trees are as unique as the other plants of the area. I have to include the paloverde (*Cercidium Torreyanum*), with its yellow blooms followed by bare green branches. The ironwood tree (*Olneya Tesota*) has pink flowers that resemble sweet peas. In my imagination, I fill in with shrubs such as the creosote bush (*Larrea tridentata*) and mesquite (*Prosopis*). Exotic flowering vines like bougainvillea and Arabian jasmine (*Jasminum Sambac*) might need a bit more water than the rest, but they are gorgeous spilling over the adobe wall. In the desert sun, the bright colors clash beautifully with the dark purple flowers of the indigo bush (*Dalea Greggii*) and the bright yellow of the prostrate *Acacia redolens*, hugging the rocks at their feet.

What would an Arizona garden be without cactus? Less prickly, but I would plant a couple of phallic-looking ones, just because I like them. And some have gorgeous flowers to boot.

Flowering penstemon grow well in the desert, so I would use plenty of those, along with yarrow (*Achillea millefolium*), set against the thick fleshy leaves of stonecrop (*Sedum*), the lacier gray wormwood (*Artemesia*), and drought-tolerant herbs like thyme and oregano. Other flowering plants suitable for this garden include the arroyo lupine (*Lupinus succulentus*), the yellow-orange California poppy (*Eschscholzia californica*), African daisy (*Dimorphotheca aurantiaca*), showy primrose (*Oenothera speciosia*), and the cheery Mexican hat (*Ratibida columnaris*).

Most of the uncultivated areas of this garden would be paved with sand, stones, and gravel, but if I wanted a patch of lawn, I would use dry-climate-tolerant Bermuda grass.

This garden would hardly ever need watering, and I think it would be lovely in the way that anything harmonious is beautiful.

Remember, the most important aspect of a garden is not the specific plants but the structures, the setting, and the overall health of whatever is growing there. Your "English cottage–style garden" does not have to contain only plants that grow well in England, any more than your house has to be a wattle-and-daub, thatch-roofed cottage, or you have to come from Slithy-Toes-upon-Twee in Sherwood Forest.

The informal "spirit of the cottage garden" is what we want to maintain, the idea that we can grow a wide variety of happy plants that we don't have to coddle, spray, or placate. That is why we want to use the right plants, and put them in the best place in the yard.

THE DEARLY DEPARTED

Inevitably some plants will languish or even die in your garden. Don't be upset by this. If nothing else, your failures will help you learn what to avoid and may save thousands of dollars in the future. I know this is true because of something that happened just the other day. Potting up some hyacinths for forcing, I was rummaging through my flowerpot collection looking for some crocking. I keep broken dishes and broken flowerpots inside empty flowerpots. I don't know why. I save broken dishes because I have this idea that one day I will make a gorgeous mosaic stone path out of them. This is a fantasy. I can't even knit, much less do Byzantine stonework. But I comfort myself with the thought that they will have an artistic heavenly afterlife.

Once I broke a lovely jade green Art Deco vase that was a gift from our friends Jo and Don. Now it sits in an old flowerpot, waiting for Byzantium.

Next to that flowerpot was one filled with plant tags—you know, those plastic labels you are supposed to put in the ground next to the plant when you install the specimen so you can identify it later. I never use them, but I don't throw them away either, which is why they were jammed in the flowerpot. There must have been thirty-five plant labels, but almost none of those plants were now growing in my garden! *Amsonia*, what happened to you? *Brunnera macrophylla, Helleborus foetidus, Delphinium* 'Connecticut Yankee', *Geum* 'Mrs. Bradshaw', where are you? Where were they? I must have lost them all, killed them!

I read *Enkianthus campanulatus,* neatly printed on a wooden label. Such a beautiful name, like a Greek actor in a tragedy by Sophocles. The red-vein enkianthus is a superb shrub with yellowish to pale orange lily-of-the-valley-like flowers in midspring. But alas, Zeus! It prefers slightly acid soil, so it reached its tragic end in the back of my garden, as the chorus wept in a stylized manner.

I confess! I, the woman laughingly known as "Mrs. Greenthumbs," have wasted thousands of dollars and killed hundreds of plants. I bet that makes you feel good.

BENIGN NEGLIGENCE

Benign negligence is the art of letting the garden do what it wants, but does not mean letting your yard turn into a weedy mess. That would be criminal negligence (at least a misdemeanor in most municipalities). It means taking note of which plants do better than others, observing the effect of the shade of a tree upon the plants beneath, moving a plant around to find the best place for it to flourish—or leaving it alone when it has found its own good place. This attention to the garden's own rhythms develops a sensitivity to nature that is essential to the making of a first-rate gardener.

If something likes to seed itself all over the garden, let it. Not teenage boys, but plants, you know what I mean.

Benign negligence is useful up to the point at which malignant cutting back and hostile weeding must begin. This takes more self-discipline than you'd think. The object here is to guide the natural progress of the garden's maturity the way you would guide a teenager's, with a firm but loving hand and an eagle eye. That means you may have to ruthlessly yank out a healthy plant that interferes with its neighbor, or weed paths by hand so that only an artistic amount of alyssum is coming up here and there. It means letting aggressive plants thrive, but taking the spade to them every couple of years when they threaten to overwhelm.

The great danger is that some of the plants that do especially well in your area will do *too* well. The wonderful blue New England aster that I saved from the developer's bulldozer promptly ravished Alma Potschke, a hybrid aster with hot pink flowers and a neater growth habit. The first year after I planted that wild New England aster, I noticed that Alma had a couple of blue flowers in the clump. Charming.

Three years later, there were no more pink asters! They were all lavender-blue. Okay, I can't very well say I was terribly upset about it. You can't have too many blue flowers in August and September. But be prepared. If you grow species with wild, unimproved genetic material, there is a good chance they will sexually molest your man-made hybrids. Not that the hybrids complain. On the contrary, they seem perfectly willing to submit to the domination of the dominant gene. There are personal ads in the paper for people like this.

Since then, the blue asters have formed huge clumps with the odd pink flower cluster here and there. Every plant has its place and an aggressive but beautiful wildflower like the New England aster is just the sort of plant to put in the empty strip between the sidewalk and the street.

I left most of my self-sown clumps of asters, but instead of replanting or giving away the rest, I dug up some and sold them at the local plant exchange, held every June at Charles and Norman's house. I rent a booth from them. What a great business it is! My stock of perennials is courtesy of Mother Nature, and selling them is so easy it feels like a scam.

THE HUDSON VALLEY PLANT SALE

Every town should have a plant sale like we have. It has been going on for about seven years now and has become quite a local event. Our host, Norman P., is a doctor and tireless worker on behalf of restoring the historic parts of town. Norman organizes the event, calls the exhibitors, and sends out the posters. Charles B. is in his fifties, with a white beard, rosy cheeks, and twinkling blue eyes that make him resemble a fit Santa in gardening clothes. I suspect that if he put on a tuxedo, he would look very distinguished. Charles's magnificent garden has been featured in *Horticulture* magazine, and it is impressive. It consists of a series of rooms. An enclosed dooryard garden featuring flowers in blue and yellow leads to a red garden, beyond which is a rock garden, nearby a cutting garden, and finally a wild garden. It is high-class horticulture and my thumbnail description does not begin to do it justice. Suffice it to say that there's never a weed in sight! It is open to the public on the day of the sale.

On the morning of the sale, private gardeners, garden clubs, and local nurseries bring their plants in trucks, station wagons, and in the trunks of cars like our old Ponti. The vendors then set up their wares in two long lines of display areas on either side of a long driveway that leads to the house and gardens.

The plant sale opens officially at 9 A.M., but by 8:30, the cognoscenti are lined up, ready to get the first crack at some new hybrid lobelia or oddball salvia. As soon as Norman raises the driveway gate, the mad gardeners actually dash out toward the vendors like greyhounds.

Dave J., an old pal of Handsome Richard and the most dedicated chain-smoker I've ever met, comes all the way from Pennsylvania with potted-up divisions of his collection of rare and old-fashioned shrubs and perennials. In a smoke-damaged voice reminiscent of Talullah Bankhead if she were a man (some say she was), he talks me into buying at least one of these unusual ones each year. I remember them fondly as I review his plant labels in my flowerpot, which are handwritten on classy wooden sticks and still smell faintly of tobacco.

Charles B. himself offers seedlings of annuals and biennials that you never see in commercial garden centers. He orders all those seeds that I can only drool over in the Thompson and Morgan catalog and grows them in his greenhouse especially for the sale. I love to buy little plants of dreamboats like Champagne Bubbles poppies (*Papaver nudicaule*), or Scotch thistle (*Onopordum acanthium*), a huge thistle with gray-white stems shaped like an Addams Family candelabrum. Some of these plants have done well and reseeded themselves, but the rest . . . in the plant-label graveyard pot.

Last year, I bought a rodgersia (*Rodgersia pinnota*) from Robert J., a well-known garden painter who has a booth at the sale. It lived. Rodgersia—its name commemorates Commodore Rodgers of the United States Navy—is a fine, shade-loving perennial that has leaves shaped like very large hands with short pointy fingers. They emerge green but turn a bronzy color later in the season. It really is a remarkable plant and is dramatic in the semi-wild area near the Greek urn.

Tim Steinhoff, the head gardener of Montgomery Place, a historic house and garden in the area, has an elegant selection of plants, which he cultivates in the garden's greenhouse. He has a special weakness for nice-smelling flowers like sweet violets (*Viola odorata*), mignonette (*Reseda odorata*), and heliotrope (*Helioropium aborescens*). So do I.

Local garden clubs are represented as well. Most of the plant offerings are divisions taken from the gardens of the members, like hybrid daylilies, hostas, monardas, and phlox. It is pretty obvious that the garden club members have brought their surplus perennials to sell, just as I do with my lustiest plants. If I were just starting out, I would head for these booths first. These hardy plants are the mainstays of the flower border—the salt of the earth, so to speak.

I'm proud to say that the "Mrs. Greenthumbs" booth has some of the cheapest plants in the sale. I don't care about filthy lucre. I only want to make enough so I can do a little shopping and buy a rare (and possibly doomed) new specimen from Dave or Charles. My most popular sales leaders are sweet autumn clematis (*Clematis terniflora*), butterfly bush (*Buddleia Davidii*), Russian sage (*Perovskia atriplicifolia superba*), and my book, which I autograph personally. At the end of the day, I give away what I haven't sold.

REAPING MOTHER NATURE'S BOUNTY

It's not me who is generous, but Mother Nature. There are some plants that self-sow so enthusiastically I know they should be weeded, but they are so attractive that I don't have the heart. Forget-me-not (*Myosotis*), foxglove (*Digitalis*), daisy (*Chrysanthemum maximum*), feverfew (*Matricaria*), sweet william (*Dianthus barbatus*), flowering tobacco (*Nicotiana alata*), opium poppy (*Papaver somniferum*), and alyssum (*Lobu-*

laria maritima)—to name a very few out of multitudes—are impossible to rip from the bosom of Mother Earth without qualms. Whenever possible, I try to sell them or give them away instead of throwing them on the compost heap.

Just about any plant will sow itself if the conditions are favorable. You often see shrubs propagate themselves from suckers. But the butterfly bush, rose-of-Sharon (*Hibiscus syriacus*), and the oak leaf hydrangea (*Hydrangea quercifolia*) have appeared from seed in my garden. The buddleias expecially love to germinate in the spaces between the flagstones. When I spot one, I lift the stone and transplant that baby right into the flower bed or flowerpot. I also sell my seedlings at Charles and Norman's plant exchange for three bucks each. This is especially delightful since at the garden center, buddleias cost about twenty bucks each! I call that free enterprise, or at least cheap enterprise.

Sometimes self-sown seedlings can be disappointing. I was thrilled when a hybrid peony seeded itself without my assistance, but the self-sown child of the beautiful hybrid had muddy pink flowers that looked like feather dusters and smelled like them, too. It's ugly, but I haven't had the heart to rip it out. Not yet.

The sweet alyssum springs up from between the stones in the path every spring. That's why they call it spring. I yank out all but a few artistic tufts, two to the right, one on the left, one near the center a little farther on, and that's it. Everything else goes into the compost unless I can find a willing neighbor to take them. It doesn't pay to pot them up and try to sell them at the sale. The knowledgeable customers aren't *that* gullible.

Some annuals, like the spider flower (*Cleome spinosa*), self-sow so neurotically I wonder how they survived before they were cultivated. When left to their own devices, they sprout all together and compete with their siblings so viciously that they form clumps of feeble stems barely a foot high with puny flowers at the end. The seedlings must be separated and ruthlessly thinned to a foot apart. Only then will they reach their full potential and grow into well branched four-foot plants with pink-and-white flowers that remind me more of fireworks than spiders. The necessity of dividing and thinning them surprises me. If they always come up so prodigiously and competitively, how do they survive in the wild? Were they one-foot-tall scrawny clumps when first discovered, and did they surprise and thrill the first botanist who cultivated them separately? (Look this up.)

I have noticed this propensity to choke one another in many self-sown plants and have wondered about it. What was nature thinking? Does nature think? What do you think?

(I looked up cleome and found out that it is native to tropical and North America, and in the West is called Rocky Mountain bee plant, also known as stinking clover. I've noticed that it does stink when cut. Otherwise, no mention of its foolish seeding habits, although cultural recommendations are to thin it heavily. I could have told you that. I *did* tell you that.)

BUT DON'T USE PLANTS THAT ARE <u>TOO</u> EASY TO GROW

I probably don't need to tell you this. In most of temperate North America, there are literally thousands of plants that will grow in our gardens without assistance. In fact, they grow everywhere without our assistance. We call them weeds, or sometimes "serial killers" when they threaten everything else in the garden. Many of them are natives that grew here long before Europeans ever set foot on shore. Many others are originally from other temperate regions, but have adapted to our climate so successfully they have made a nuisance of themselves.

By advocating growing what grows easily, I'm not suggesting that we should encourage criminals at the expense of more interesting or better behaved plants—the results can be disastrous.

The previous owner of my garden, an old man who raised pigeons in the back, planted Japanese bamboo (*Polygonum cuspidatum*) in the side yard in the 1950s. This stuff, also known as knotweed, is twelve feet high and propagates itself by division, seed, root cuttings, and, I suspect, assault and battery, arson, and extortion.

Knotweed is the most indestructible plant I have ever met. Walter dug it up, cut it in pieces, mutilated it, and threw it into the landfill behind the Buffalo's Club parking lot. He lobbed the pieces out as far as he could, rotating before finally discharging the missile, like an Olympic discus thrower. A few weeks later, a Buffalo dumped a load of concrete rubble over the clump of knotweed roots and we left it for dead.

The next summer, there was knotweed coming up through the concrete. This Rasputin sent out its handsome leaves and tall stalks as though it were still growing in the yard, as though its roots were still attached to something, as though it couldn't care less! It was frightening. Beware Japanese Bamboo! It's an immortal alien that will take over your yard, perhaps your life.

The old man who used to own our house planted it on purpose, thinking he was getting himself an easy-to-grow plant, just the same sort of thing I'm recommending to you now. Well, I'm not recommending it. I can't in conscience condone the use of such an aggressive species for garden use. We all know the story of the kudzu vine's intrusions in southern farmlands, the Hall's honeysuckle (*Lonicera japonica Halliana*) that chokes out woodlands in the Northeast, the purple loosestrife that has invaded wetlands across the country. There is a limit to how well even I want a plant to do. Let me warn you about gooseneck loosestrife (*Lysimachia clethroides*), old man (*Artemesia Abrotanum*), and any other plant that has stoloniferous, or creeping, roots. Grow them, but watch them and be prepared to pull.

BUT DON'T USE PLANTS THAT ARE <u>TOO</u> HARD TO GROW

Most of us try them, those rarefied, sissified exotics that have to be mollycoddled, nursed along, watered, and given even more tender loving care than my whining, drug-addicted viburnum. Of course I'm talking about none other than the nation's favorites: hybrid petunias, marigolds, and all the other annuals found at local garden centers and roadside farm stands.

Okay, before you kill me, these plants are perfect for window boxes and to fill in between perennials. By themselves, more often than not these small plants are all out of proportion to a house, a path, a group of shrubs, or any object bigger than a bread box. My other objection is ecological. These plants are originally tropical and require a heated greenhouse and an industrial operation to produce them for market. And because they are so poorly adapted to the North American climate, they can't reseed themselves; you have to buy new ones every year, which is the horticultural equivalent of built-in obsolescence. Are we suckers, or what?

The other most popular plant in America is the hybrid tea rose. Hybrid teas are the three D's of the plant world: Difficult, Demanding, and Dead. They need to be fed, watered, mulched, sprayed, covered in winter, and pruned in some arcane ceremony at just the right moment in the spring. Yes, I've grown them myself. Who can resist a rose? But I only buy them when they go on sale for two dollars around July 15, and I don't give them any special treatment.

A few high-maintenance plants are all right in a cottage garden, but all across the country you see house after house with nothing but petunias and hybrid tea roses in the yard. The reason for the popularity of these plants is that unlike perennials, which are usually small green plants at the time of purchase, industrially grown annuals and roses are in full bloom, on the table in the nursery, at the beginning of May. In my area, that is the time of the most feverish garden activity, when homeowners start mowing their lawns and the nice weather makes them want to get out and "do something" in the yard. Professional owners of garden centers know that flowering annuals sell better than small green perennials and there is a good reason for it.

It is a well-known scientific fact that flowers are the sexual organs of plants. We also know this instinctively. On St. Valentine's Day, nobody gives their sweetheart stems and leaves. No one says, "I love you, darling, here's a root!" No, we give flowers because we understand their true psychological significance. So it comes as no surprise that most of us find flowers almost irresistibly attractive. I would venture to say that flowers are some of the most beautiful sexual organs I've ever seen. Then again, I haven't been around all that much.

There is a compromise between introducing a thug like the knotweed and squandering good money and time on exotic hybrids and annuals, and that is to plant what you like and what likes you.

4

Have Something in Bloom
Throughout the Gardening
Season

THE EVERBLOOMING BORDER is to cottage gardeners what the Pulitzer Prize is to authors, the Oscar is to movie actors—the laurel, the plum, the giant zucchini of success. A garden that resembles a half-acre bouquet at all times during the gardening season, loaded with flowers, berries, vines, and fruits is the perfumed, color-filled fantasy of every one of us. Many attempt but few accomplish this lofty goal.

An everblooming garden is like a painting in motion. The succession of bloom from spring to fall is fascinating to observe as the colors change with each passing week. The French Impressionist Claude Monet tried to capture this fleeting art of nature by painting the same spot at different days and seasons, and the results were breathtaking. The real thing is even better.

A lot of people think so, for instance my neighbor Minnie Abulafian. She's a heavy-set woman who wears tight pink jogging pants that match her pink hair rollers as she walks her Chihuahua past my house every morning. She tells me she loves to note each day what new plant is blooming, and to admire the "ever-changing panorama of color," as she puts it. All right, she's no *New York Times* art critic, I admit, but she appreciates the changing quality of nature's (and my) handiwork for all the right reasons. Sometimes she indicates that she would love to see the back garden as well, maybe stop in for a cup of coffee, but I don't take the hint. I just thank her for the compliment and give her pooch a gentle shove to keep it from whizzing on my nasturtiums.

Like millions of other cottage gardeners, I have lulls. In the hot weather after the big June crescendo, my garden relaxes into a shriveled, languid, damp diminuendo, as tousled as a motel bed the morning after a torrid one-night stand. The peonies, the irises, the roses, and the mock oranges are finished blooming; the summer flowers—the Asiatic lilies, daylilies, bee balm, and daisies are still contemplating opening their buds.

At that moment my garden is Dullsville.

It's times like these when all the garden books tell you to depend on foliage and form. Which to me is like saying, "You failed." Of course, a well-designed garden has interesting leaf color and form, and borders that feature contrasting leaves are admirable in a polite, restrained, chaste kind of way. But a cottage garden in bloom flaunts itself like a parade float.

Taking my own advice about finding the right plant for the right place, I looked around the neighborhood to see what was blooming during my lull. Perhaps I was missing a perfectly obvious specimen that would tide me over beautifully. There were a few late roses around town, some rhododendrons, and mountain laurels (*Kalmia latifolia*) in the cooler, higher elevations nearby, but that was about it. Rhododendrons and mountain laurels turn yellow and expire in my yard because my soil is not acidic enough. It was then that I became determined to learn some ways to keep the garden blooming at all times. And since then, I have discovered some techniques that . . .

SOME EXCEPTIONS

All right, all right, not everyone *has* to have an everblooming garden. There are certain circumstances in which it is either impossible or undesirable. Some gardens are time-sensitive no matter how well planned they are, and by their very nature can bloom only for a few weeks a year. Woodland gardens are at their best in the spring, and desert gardens bloom after the rains come, no matter what you do.

And there are special gardens whose creators have a special purpose. Before I go on to tell you how to make an everblooming garden, let me tell you about one that makes giving up a long season worth it.

THE MOST BEAUTIFUL ROSE GARDEN I'VE EVER SEEN

One of the great English gardens I visited on my TV tour was Elsing Hall, famous for its old-fashioned roses. Unlike modern hybrid roses, these antique beauties act like other shrubs in that they have one blooming period and do "it" all at once in a big flush, and then it's over. These roses are covered with bloom in shades of soft pink, white, and a purple pink that rosarians call "rose madder" in early summer, and then they quit flowering completely and sensibly concentrate on making leaves and hips for the rest of the season. Not everything wonderful can last forever; in fact, some of the greatest moments of our lives last but a few seconds (see "Climaxing" on page 139).

The flowering time of old roses in England is not as fleeting as you might suspect. In the cool, slow English growing season, these roses start blooming in early June, and look good even in the second week of July, which is when I saw them. In our hot, hot North American summers, old-fashioned roses "go over" much more quickly, so a garden devoted to old roses is less rewarding here, except in the Pacific Northwest, which, as we've said, resembles the British Isles in climate.

Shirley Cargill's rose garden at Elsing Hall was not at all like those rose beds that you see in municipal parks. There were no stiff rows of hybrid teas in contrasting colors, neatly mulched with wood chips. No, these roses were in a climate where they grew easily and their happiness was proclaimed by their abundance.

Roses cascaded over the stone walls of the fifteenth-century manor house and ran riot down an embankment to a moat covered with water lilies. The place looked like an illustration for *Idylls of the King,* by Tennyson. In fact, I could almost imagine the Lady of Shalott, who was in love with Sir Lancelot, floating down to Camelot in her waterlogged bier, having expired for love. For the show, I eased gingerly into a tiny flat-bottomed boat that was moored to a tree next to the moat, tied a scarf around my head and pretended to be the Lady of Shalott myself. The boat was pretty leaky, and I almost sank into the watery mire, having expired for the camera.

It was just the kind of garden that inspired such folly. This garden looked "natural" and "wild."

While we're on the subject, I have a word to say about "natural" gardens. The difference between a "wild" garden and a "wild-looking" garden is not in the word *wild*, but in the word *looking*. This "wild-looking" garden required much more planning

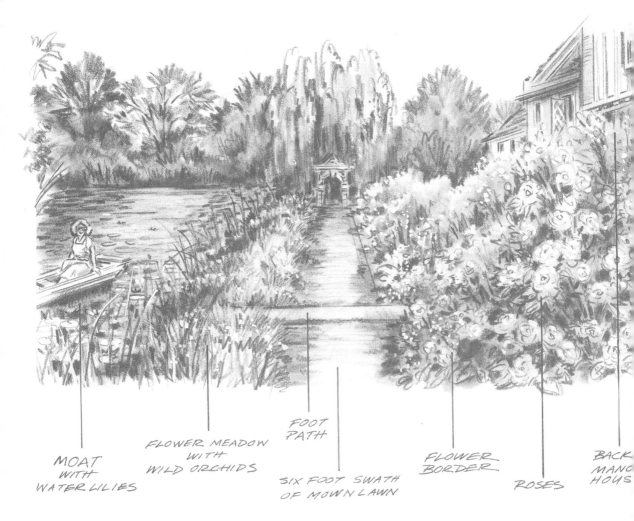

MOAT
WITH
WATER LILIES

FLOWER MEADOW
WITH
WILD ORCHIDS

FOOT
PATH

SIX FOOT SWATH
OF MOWN LAWN

FLOWER
BORDER

ROSES

BACK
MANO
HOUS

and care than any of those pine-bark-mulched beds of hybrid teas in public parks. It takes at least as much cultivation, maybe more, to maintain just the right amount of abundance and still be able to see everything.

I learned a great deal from Shirley Cargill. (I love that this lady was named Shirley. She was nothing like any Shirley I have ever known in Brooklyn, let me tell you. For example, no Shirley in Brooklyn ever used the phrase "quite extraordinary!") Shirley had hundreds of rambling roses growing up two-story garden walls. They looked as if they just happened to grow there, but I knew better. I asked her about it.

At first she denied doing much of anything to them. Part of the mystique of the "wild" garden is the notion that the gardener doesn't really do anything. You hear this from advocates of "natural," "native" gardens in this country, and it's a crock. "Wild-looking" means you don't have to cultivate anything, they imply. And "natural" really puts them on the high moral/ecological ground. The word *natural* has come to have a positive meaning not too far from the word *holy.* "Natural goodness" is a virtue most often used in connection with breakfast cereal (which, by the way, is manufactured), but I recently heard a TV minister end a benediction with the words, "May natural goodness be with you always. Amen." (What does that mean? Throw away your clothes and go native?)

"Come on, Shirley, this didn't all happen by chance," I chided. "Otherwise we'd all do nothing and our gardens would all look this great."

"It's quite extraordinary, isn't it?" she murmured coyly.

"Don't give me that again. What do you do to keep this up?"

"Not much."

"Oh, Shirley, please, please," I begged shamelessly.

"All right, all right, but you must never tell anyone."

I promised without batting an eye.

"Each spring, I spend twelve hours a day, every day for a month, hacking those ramblers back. It's a devil of a task. They scratch me, branches fall on my head, leaving me bloody and in terrible pain. But it's worth it, I tell you, worth it."

She was right. It was worth it. Here are some of the tricks I dragged out of Mrs. Cargill that make a garden appear both wild and neat at the same time:

1. At the back of the house facing the moat, Shirley had a deep flower border. Until she bought the manor house, there had been a conventional broad lawn between this border and the moat, a tidy but dull solution to a stretch of ground leading to water. Then one day a friend of hers noticed the leaves of wild spotted orchids (*Dactylorhiza Fuchsii*) in the lawn. These are English wildflowers. That was all Shirley needed to hear. She stopped mowing immediately, just to give the orchids "a go," as she put it. When I saw it, the area between the border and the water was a flowery meadow, filled with wild orchids. But here's what made it all look artistic instead of unkempt: Between the flower border and meadow was a narrow, six-foot swath of mown lawn. Thus she had made a path to take you across the meadow without having to wade through itchy, buggy, tall grass and had a convenient area from which to tend the border. The mown area had a practical purpose, but it was very artistic as well. If the meadow had come right up to the flowers, you couldn't have seen the flowers or the meadow, because there would have been no line to separate them. That six-foot mown swath made a frame around the roses and made the meadow look deliberate, which it was.

2. Plants were allowed to grow between the cracks of the pavements, but only up to a point. Weeds were ruthlessly removed (is there a kind way to remove weeds?) and only those plants that placed themselves in the aesthetic design were allowed to remain. Miraculously, it appeared as if no plant had ever decided to grow in an area where I needed to walk.

3. Vines were encouraged to grow up walls and hang languidly over architectural features. A fragrant honeysuckle that grew on the wall was draped across the arched doorway to the manor house. The sweet smell hit you in the nose when you went out, but the branches didn't hit you in the eye; there was a lot of pruning involved.

It was, indeed, quite extraordinary. I told Shirley that the place was so sensuous, it looked as if it was wearing a negligee and was falling out of the top. I confessed it made me hot. "Oh, that's wonderful!" she exclaimed, a woman after my own heart. "That's exactly what it's supposed to do!" Which brings me quite naturally to . . .

CLIMAXING

When a garden has many different flowers all blooming at once, that is called climaxing. It means that most of the plants have reached the crescendo of their bloom at the same moment, a simultaneous climax, if you will. One big climax per season is a pretty respectable showing for an average garden, but we want more. Yes, this is *that* kind of how-to book, and I'm going to tell you how to have multiple climaxes in your garden.

My secret for having several flowering peaks per season is to use one main flowering plant for each part of the season and plant to complement it. Your main plants should probably be from your easy-to-grow list, because you want that starring plant to be surefire.

After you have found a plant that grows easily in your garden, say the daylily, let that one plant be the basis for the design. Then find other plants, bulbs, or shrubs that bloom at the same time, like the blue columns of delphiniums and bugbane (*Cimicifuga*) with its tall, deer-proof, cream-colored candles of bloom. The color and form of these plants will contrast with the daylily's.

A SEASON OF CLIMAXES

For most gardeners in North America, early spring comes between February and April. It is a tough time of year to garden, but it's just right for the witch hazel show! When I was very young, there used to be a puppet show on television called *Kukla, Fran and Ollie*. On it was a character named Witch Hazel, an old woman with a hooked beak and a bad temper. When I discovered that there was a shrub by that name, I was delighted, the way you feel when you suddenly make a connection between two previously unrelated worlds. Luckily for our purposes, the shrub is more attractive than the puppet. Witch hazel (*Hamamelis*) has several varieties, and they all bloom somewhere between December and April.

In my climate, the witch hazel *Hamemelis* x *intermedia* blooms in late March with delicately fragrant yellow blossoms that look like the tufts on a chenille bedspread.

There are precious few plants to accompany this oddball shrub, so I use whatever I can.

I plant groups of hellebores (*Helleborus niger*), with creamy pink nodding bells, in front of the witch hazel, which go nicely with snowdrops (*Galanthus nivalis*) and the bright yellow buttercups of winter aconite (*Eranthis hyemalis*), along with species crocus in yellow, white, and lavender-blue. There's a good chance that the witch hazel will bloom and finish before even the early spring bulbs get going, but that's the chance you take at this time of year, so get used to it. It's impressive to have anything at all. In the South you have many more plants to choose from and you can even make midwinter gardens using witch hazel, along with other winter-blooming plants, like jasmine (*Jasminum nudiflorum*).

In early May, the Henry lilacs (*Syringa* x *Henryi*) in my front yard have always been a source of inspiration. There are three very large specimens, averaging about fifteen feet wide and twelve feet tall, and when in bloom these rare lilacs dominate the garden, to say the least. Their loose panicles are pinker than the common lilac and much larger, up to a foot long, and the heart-shaped leaves are smaller. I don't know why you can't buy this variety at the local garden center, but I've only seen it advertised once, in the upscale Winterthur catalog. I would like to feel superior for growing it, but the bushes were there when I bought my old house.

If I never planted anything else in the yard, these lilacs would still provide plenty of bloom for spring, but, I said to myself, when you have such an opportunity to gild the lily, so to speak, it seems a shame not to take it.

Thanks to the previous owners, there is also a white garland spirea (*Spiraea Thunbergii*) that flowers at the same time in the borders leading up to the front door. Its slender arching branches, clad in what look like thousands of teensy white rosebuds, contrast perfectly with the rounded plumpness of the lilac bushes.

Just behind the fence is a Chinese tree peony, which I planted, that frustrates me to no end. When I bought it on sale about four years ago as a one-foot stick, its label said the flowers would be dark purple. How fabulous to have a dark purple tree peony blooming in front of my lavender lilacs, I thought, artistically. It finally bloomed last year and the flowers were bright cherry red! Mislabeling is the price you pay for buying leftovers on sale, I suppose. The cherry red didn't exactly clash with the lilacs as orange would, but the yard, with its green picket fence, looked like an Easter basket.

I decided to work with it. I went to the local garden center and bought tulips in shades of pale yellow, white, a lavender-pink the same color as the lilacs, some "black" tulips, and, just to make sure it all looked deliberate, a bright cherry red variety the same color as that Chinese tree peony. I figured if the front yard was going to look like an Easter basket anyway, I'd use the tulips as jelly beans.

That winter, the deer came right down the street and ate the tulips. So last fall, I planted less palatable alliums (*Allium aflatunese*) instead. I'm looking at the garden as I write this, and I must say, the big light-purple heads of the alliums echo the lilacs brilliantly, and this year, for some reason (perhaps because of the nearness of the alliums?) the deer didn't eat all the tulips. Now all I need is a few chocolate bunnies and I'll have a real spring "look."

Incidentally, the Chinese tree peony has put out six very large, very bright blooms this year. I'm trying to get used to it, but I may just do what I always do with flowers that annoy me: I'll cut them and make a giant peony bouquet for the house. It's a no-lose situation.

If you have good luck with peonies in June, plant lots of them, even start a collection. That way, you will be assured of a brilliant show during peony-flowering season, which is from May to June depending on the part of the country you live in. Once you have a leading plant like the peony, you are ready to hire the supporting cast. Plant a lacy June-blooming shrub, like the bridal wreath spirea (*Spiraea Vanhouttei*), behind the peonies. The taller shrub's delicate white blooms are a beautiful contrast to the full, heavy peony flowers. Drifts of sweet williams (*Dianthus barbatus*) echo the color and form of the peony flowers on a much smaller scale. Bluebells (*Campanula*) add their blue color and graceful form. Now you have four plants blooming during the late spring, early summer season, making a garden picture for that time. There are many more plants you could add, but simply planting lots of these few will create a sense of abundance.

All right, peony season is easy. How can you go wrong in June with roses, peonies, irises, and all those flowering shrubs to choose from? But July brings the plants of high summer, the hollyhocks (*Althaea rosea*), daylilies (*Hemerocallis*), tiger lilies (*Lilium tigrinum*), and luscious Aurelian lilies that fill the late afternoon air with their heady perfume. At the same time, the butterfly bush (*Buddleia Davidii*) gets going, its airiness contrasting with the substance of the lilies and summer-flowering clematis. I don't hesitate to combine these plants with daisies, Queen Anne's lace, and other wildflowers of summer.

By August, the surrounding countryside is full of wildflowers that often look better than the garden. There is nothing unethical about incorporating a common wildflower into the cultivated garden. Foolish, perhaps. Wildflowers, or weeds, as they used to be called before the days of ecological correctness, have the advantage of being easy to grow (perhaps too easy!). A weed . . . uh, wildflower . . . grown in the company of a few high-society hybrid perennials has all the enthusiasm of the nouveau riche at a debutante ball. Just be prepared to yank out any wildflower that becomes aggressive.

Last year, mistaking a large clump of narrow goldenrod (*Solidago*) leaves for those of a hybrid aster, I allowed a big specimen to grow unimpeded in the flower border that flanks my front walk. By late summer when it began to bloom, it had reached six feet, thanks to good garden soil. It looked so stately I didn't have the heart to dig it out, and it went so well with the other plants I had there! There was the amaranth (*Amaranthus elegantissimus*), an eight-foot-tall annual related to the Central American grain plant. It has large maroon leaves and maroon seed heads that resemble thick, heavy ostrich plumes. I obtained my first amaranth seeds by taking a cluster from a plant in the garden of an early employer, a cheap bastard who wanted a magenta garden. But that is another story. (In fact, I told it in my previous book, *Mrs. Greenthumbs*. . . .) In any case, the tasseled goldenrod flowers, together with the plumes of the red-purple amaranth, were an interesting and unique combination. Complemented by airy, daisy-like white boltonias and yellow and tangerine nasturtiums—only modesty prevents me from calling it absolutely beautiful.

And thus the lowly field goldenrod was transformed into a cultivated garden perennial, the centerpiece of my late summer front garden. There will come a time when the goldenrod tries to take over, and yes, I will call the bouncer (my shovel) and have it ruthlessly thrown out. Until then, I will enjoy nature's bounty. (Incidentally, the

American goldenrod is a prized garden plant in Europe. They even hybridize them and pay money for them. Go figure.)

In fall, the leaves of the burning bush (*Euonymus americanus*) turn a cherry red so brilliant, they're impossible to ignore. One might be tempted just to tiptoe away and leave the garden to its own devices when such a loud member is shouting, but the cherry red leaves of the burning bush would sound more like singing if it were accompanied by graceful flowers of Japanese anemones (*Anemone japonica*) floating on their tall wiry stems in shades of pink and white. Fat mauve chrysanthemums, those airy-fairy white boltonias and asters such as Harrington's Pink, or Alma Potschke, all of which bloom at the same time as the burning bush, would also lighten and soften the flaming red chorus. What a symphonic climax!

As we can see, a shrub makes a terrific starting place for a climax. And since a cottage garden is one where shrubs and herbaceous perennials are mixed with abandon, a large shrub will dominate the scene when it is in flower, if only because it's so big. You can design a climax around any favorite garden plant, even something as tiny as the primrose, but it helps to have a noble grand shrub for each part of the season, just for safety, not to mention heft, fullness, and abundance.

PLANNING A LONG-SEASON GARDEN WITH SHRUBS

Did you ever notice that the shrubs in most gardens bloom mainly in late spring? That's because those are the ones that were flowering when the gardener went shopping at the nursery during the mad flush of spring-gardening lust. It is a well-known fact in the garden center biz: Plants that bloom in the spring sell like crazy.

So don't go to the garden center and buy only what is in bloom or you'll have a garden like everybody else's, loaded with shrubs that flower in spring, but dull for the rest of the year. If you do find yourself with a mad case of spring lust (who doesn't?), just stay out of garden centers and singles bars between March and May. If you find temptation as irresistible as I do, I suggest going to the garden center in the summer and fall only, and to the bars not at all.

The surefire way to avoid having an all spring-blooming garden is to plan it backward. Start with winter and go through the seasons in reverse.

Winter

Find shrubs that look their best at this time of year, such as Tartarian dogwood (*Cornus alba sibirica*) with twiggy bright red branches. It's a true shrub, unlike the dogwood tree we are used to seeing. Members of the Cotoneaster family, some of which are evergreen, have colorful winter berries, and don't forget holly for Christmastime. In southern areas, you lucky stiffs have evergreen skimmia (*Skimmia japonica*) with shiny leaves and big red berries, as well as winter-blooming yellow jasmine (*Jasminum nudiflorum*) and many other shrubs. Evergreens are a winter must, but don't plant only evergreens or the result will be equally dreary all year-round.

Autumn

The peegee hydrangea (*Hydrangea paniculata grandiflora*) holds on to its big pouffes of mauve-pink blooms well into the fall. Shrub roses have spectacular red hips. Some look like berries; some look like crab apples. Pay attention to a plant's autumn leaf color, like that previously mentioned burning bush. Garden author Allen Lacy's favorite tree in autumn is the native sourwood (*Oxydendron arboreum*) because of its cherry red fall foliage combined with cream-colored seed heads. His favorite shrub is the oak-leafed hydrangea (*Hydrangea quercifolia*) when its leaves turn shades of dark red, crimson, and rust. He calls them, "a good shade of coppery red brushed with wine."* Whatever you call it, the color is fabulous and as rich-looking as dark red morocco leather. I was happy to read that he also loved the purple smoke bush (*Cotinus*), because it is one of my favorites, as well.

---

*Allen Lacy, *The Garden in Autumn* (New York: Atlantic Monthly Press, 1990).

Summer

It's August, time to go to the garden center and see what's in bloom. Even better, see what's on sale. Ah, here is the hydrangea, sweet pepperbush (*Clethra alnifolia*), and rose-of-Sharon (*Hisbiscus*). I have several pink rose-of-Sharon shrubs and I'm very fond of them. I know a lot of people who are snobbish about this bush, especially the pink-flowered variety, probably because it is commonly grown in Brooklyn and it is often combined with orange marigolds by unsophisticated gardeners. This sickening combination of colors contributes to its unpopularity in haute horticultural circles. I like the rose-of-Sharon because it's a big substantial plant with lots of hibiscus-type flowers and it blooms in August, when most other plants are conking out. If the pink one is too Brooklyn for you, there are white- and blue-flowered versions available. Snob.

July is the month of the butterfly bush with its seven-foot fountain of flowers, and in the warmer parts of the country, the tender, purple-flowered chaste tree (*Vitex Agnus-castus*).

June in one word: roses. In two words: even more. This is the June garden with its overflow of white-flowering shrubs like the showy six-foot deutzia (*Deutzia scabra*), the beautifully fragrant mock orange (*Philadelphus coronarius*), the greenish soccer balls of the Annabelle hydrangea (*Hydrangea arborescens* 'Annabelle'). The beauty bush (*Kolkwitzia amabilis*) comes in white and shades of pink. There are also the colorful potentillas in red and yellow and pink, and of course the large Rhododendron family gets going. If you have no shrubs blooming in your garden in June, get some from a neighbor. Everybody's got something.

Spring

Last of all, choose shrubs for spring, but if you have run out of room, don't worry. Since everyone else's yard will be screaming with yellow forsythias and magenta azaleas, their eyes will be too blinded to notice any omission in yours.

This is how cottage gardeners impress each other: They invite one another to dinner when everything in the garden is blooming its head off.

"Can you and Walter came over for dinner on June third?" asked my friend Peggy R. recently.

"June third?" Resting the phone on my ear, I checked my engagement book, even though I knew it was blank. "Let me see . . ."

"Not June tenth!" she added, with unnatural anxiety in her voice, before I even had a chance to answer. "I'm . . . I'm going to be at . . . at my sister's house that week!"

I knew very well that this was a lie, and she knew I knew. She wasn't going to her sister's, any more than I was going to Paris. She lives with her sister. But I didn't say anything. I understood. "Sure, the third will be fine," I agreed, glad to get a dinner invitation, even when accompanied by a fib. I understood that on June third, her peonies and irises would be at the peak of their glory, and by the next week, finished. I understood that it is the rare gardener who is able to invite people every week of the gardening season. I understood her necessity.

I've had cruel neighbors drop in at odd times, just to catch my garden in the act of not blooming. And when I just happen to innocently drop in on somebody else's garden, and when I hear for the fifty-thousandth time, "Oh, you should have seen it last week!" I know they're telling the truth.

Some people get around the problem by devoting a different area of the garden to each month of the gardening season and letting the rest go. Gertrude Jekyll did this on a large scale. Each of her garden rooms was devoted to one season only. She had a spring garden of bulbs surrounding an old well, a 120-foot-long summer-flowering border, which she kept in constant bloom by replacing plants from her private nursery, and a garden of asters and gray-leaved plants that bloomed only in September. Because each area was separated from the rest by hedges and walls, it would have been easy for her to lead guests only into the area that looked colorful and ignore the rest, sort of like a hostess with only one clean room.

For most of us, Miss Jekyll's solution is futile, since we don't have garden rooms defined by high outdoor walls. It would be impossible to get a guest to ignore the rest of my garden short of blindfolding him, leading him to a chair facing the blooming part of the garden, and strapping him in so he couldn't look anywhere else. I have had guests whom I suspect would enjoy this treatment.

USING CONTAINER PLANTS TO FILL IN LULLS

In classic English garden books, it is recommended that you use potted plants to fill in spaces in the perennial border. They are supposed to be grown elsewhere, out of sight of the public or the lord of the manor, and then brought forth at just the moment of perfect bloom. I would love to do that. Most of us have neither the time, the space, nor an employer to pay us to grow a wide array of plants that are seen only in full bloom. I've tried to do it myself without a greenhouse, and it's very difficult.

I learned my lesson from the chimney bellflower (*Campanula pyramidalis*). It is a biennial with a magnificent, five-foot purple spire that blooms the second year. But like most biennials, the first year it is a boring little tuft of leaves. One year I started them from seed and waited until the following summer for the little tufts to bloom. I must say they were beautiful, and they did what they were supposed to do, fill in summer lulls. But since they didn't self-sow in my yard, I realized I would have to go through the whole seedling process again every year, so regretfully I gave up.

Last spring I found some year-old, ready-to-flower chimney bellflower plants at Charles and Norman's plant sale. They were three dollars each! Quite a chunk of change for a plant that would bloom only once for about a month and then vanish forever. I bought five and they bloomed this year and were sensational again. But fifteen bucks for a quick trip to the moon on gossamer wings was too much.

My practical solution is to grow annuals in containers. The great virtue of annuals is that they bloom all season. Petunias, impatiens, salvias, dusty millers, lobelias, marigolds, and the rest of the ubiquitous annuals from the garden center and the supermarket look skimpy in the garden but wonderful in pots. The small size of a six-pack of French marigolds is in much better proportion to a flowerpot than it is to a four-by-twelve-foot flower border in front of the house.

Most of the time, I keep my pots on the steps leading to the side porch. Flowerpots on steps gain a certain importance, as though each specimen had a little stage of its own. I usually put the larger pots on the lower steps and the smaller ones higher up. You don't have to do it that way, but the effect is subtle and artistic, and that's what I live for. Since the porch steps are right near the kitchen, it is also easy to water and feed the potted annuals.

I move the pots to the flower borders to fill in when the perennials are at a lull, usually in late July or August. I don't try to sink the pots or hide them, as you are supposed to do in a traditional border. I group the pots along the path in front of the border just as I would on the porch or pergola. These groupings draw the eye away from the green behind them.

I could just plant the annuals right in the border and leave them there all summer, but then I wouldn't be able to move them to cover blanks. Sometimes I stick a big pot of annuals right over a leafless spot where I have just cut down a clump of daylilies. When the daylilies start to resprout, I move the pot. Pots are the latest gardening chic, and add architectural interest in the middle of the garden, I tell myself.

I like to use one type of annual per pot so that each one really makes a statement and I have good control over the colors. Three pots of yellow marigolds combined with two pots of blue lobelia (*pow!*) will compensate for any lack of color in the perennial border.

The most common complaint about containers is that they have to be watered very often. Well, that's right, and there's no easy way around it. If you are going away for more than a day or two, you have to ask a neighbor to water the plants for you, or call the kid who shovels the walk in winter.

My favorite containers are plain terra-cotta pots. Whenever I see them at a yard sale, I grab them, especially if they are encrusted. I love the shape, color, texture, and even the smell of old terra-cotta pots. Plants love them, too, since the porous surface mimics earth itself and assures that the plant will never die of root rot, because excess water evaporates quickly (which is why these pots have to be watered so often).

One way to deal with the watering problem is to use large pots, at least ten to twenty inches across. Don't bother with those little six-inch ones. I found a whole stack of ten-inch azalea pots that some fool was getting rid of at a yard sale. They are shorter than standard pots and I find the low center of gravity very pleasing. Not only do I use them for forcing bulbs in the winter, but the short size makes them ideal for small annuals such as violet-and-yellow Johnny-jump-ups (*Viola tricolor*), gay petunias (*Petunia hybrida*), white sweet alyssum (*Lobularia maritima*), and royal blue lobelia (*Lobelia Erinus*).

My pal Bobbie collects unusual flowerpots. It's great when people have a hobby like that because you always know what to give them on their birthday and for Christmas. Luckily, you can find wonderful terra-cotta pots all over now. I bought some really nice knockoffs of expensive Italian pots in a cheapo discount store, and Bobbie never knew the difference. They were shaped like lilies and had what looked like braided handles, all in terra-cotta. The discount store also had square terra-cotta pots with acanthus leaves in bas-relief. A Greek urn it wasn't, but it looked really nice all the same. There is a lot of junk around, but if you stick to unglazed terra cotta, you can't go wrong, and the various sizes and shapes give interest to a grouping of annuals. (Last Christmas, Bobbie informed me she had stopped collecting flowerpots and was now collecting jewelry. Was that a hint?)

I have seen annuals growing in all sorts of containers, and I don't mean plastic pots. I visited a Salvation Army thrift shop one day and came home with dozens of possibilities. Petunias in a pair of old sneakers? Amusing. Rosemary growing out of a teapot, thyme in an old clock, salvia in a 1940s vase, marigolds growing out of old wineglasses. I planted 1960s pocketbooks with ivy and pansies. They made wonderful gifts! At least no one complained about them. To my face.

You can use any object with an opening large enough to hold a plant and some soil. Containers that don't hold water, like pocketbooks, have to be lined with plastic, of course. I used plastic shopping bags from the supermarket and cut them to the right size. If the container had no hole in the bottom, I put in an inch of pebbles and warned the owner to water sparingly. Actually, the word *owner* is incorrect. I prefer to use the word *master* for the keeper of a plant, or in the case of a woman like me, *mistress*. When a plant is bought by me or given to me, I call myself the plant's mistress; take the meaning as you will.

These impromptu planters don't necessarily last too long, but they're novelty items anyway. You wouldn't want to stake your gardening reputation on such frivolities.

HOW TO KEEP THE GARDEN ABUNDANT AND EVERBLOOMING

A garden is not virtual reality. It is reality. You don't need any fancy electronic equipment to enjoy it. In fact, the closer you get to the sensory experience, the better. Making your own garden is living firsthand and there's nothing vicarious about it. The act of growing plants on your own, as opposed to seeing them growing in a magazine or visiting a public garden, is like enjoying the warm moisture of a real kiss instead of sending "xxxx" on the Internet.

A garden is nature in the raw—and it's all right there. It amazes me when people say they are going on a vacation "to see nature." You don't have to put on a backpack and go hiking in the Grand Tetons to commune with nature. The natural world is outside the kitchen door. (But not necessarily in the form of a "natural" garden, as we have noted before.) The backyard teems with life. Everything in it eats, fights, wins, loses, mates, kills, just like everywhere else on earth. I try my best to cooperate with it, so it will go in the general direction, along the general lines, of my desire. Sometimes I feel like an artist, but not one who draws from nature, or whose subject is nature, but whose medium is the action of nature itself.

The secret of the everblooming, abundant garden is in the basic bounty of the earth—rich, healthy soil. One of the best ways to achieve this beauty is to make "gardener's gold"—compost.

Oh, no, I hear you groan; here comes the lecture about the glories of rotting vegetables. I don't lecture. I nag.

Make compost . . . what's the matter with you? It is the single greatest thing you can do for the earth . . . even if you live all your life as a couch potato, even if you never do a single useful thing in your miserable existence, if you make a compost heap in the backyard, you can always say, "Leave me alone, I'm busy decomposing. . . ."

To some people, compost making is the most thrilling part of gardening. After all, the earth provides us with most of our nurture, and making a compost heap is a way of recycling some of that bounty and creating yet more fertility, health, and food for life itself. It is a righteous act and beneficial to the planet.

A famous organic gardener in Brooklyn was so delighted with his compost pile, he displayed it in the middle of the garden, like a focal point. He thought it was more beautiful than the flowers. Of course, he was cockeyed; it looked like a pile of kitchen scraps and garden debris and should have been hidden. Like a good deed, a compost heap is most virtuous when not made public.

There exists an extensive literature about making compost. In fancy compost making, all seeds of discarded vegetable matter are killed by the high temperatures created by the perfect setup. In sloppy composting, like mine, they are not. Does that mean I shouldn't compost? Of course not! Trust me, you don't need to do it by the book; the results will be wonderful just the same.

COMPOSTING FOR EVERYONE

All nature is a compost heap. Who do you think raked the fallen leaves in the forest primeval—dinosaurs?

The simplest way to make compost is to clear an area that is out of direct sunlight and out of sight. Place the heap in a shady spot behind a thick shrub, or if you don't have one in a convenient place, behind a small fence you can make yourself. A wattle screen would be adorable.

There are a number of compost bins on the market, simple chicken-wire containers that keep the pile looking neat, as well as super-efficient metal tumblers on legs, black plastic barrels with sliding panels, and white plastic aerated boxes. They're fine if you like that sort of thing, but to me they are less attractive than the heap. If I had one of those, I would hide it behind a bush.

My compost contains plenty of weed seeds, but it also contains other seeds as well. You could start a whole flower and vegetable garden from a square foot of my compost. It is full of seeds of cosmos, cleome, tomato, potato, melon, nicotiana, black-eyed susan, forget-me-not, amaranthus, snapdragon, opium poppy, hollyhock, aster, dame's rocket, and goldenrod, not to mention the weeds. You have only to spread a layer of my compost thinly on bare ground, stand back, and a whole garden of plants will appear. That's the plus side of seedy compost.

I'm sloppy, I do it wrong, and it doesn't matter.

HOW TO CREATE COMPOST

Consult composting literature for the proper way to create compost. Just kidding. It is so simple, I can tell you how to do it in three steps.

1. Collect kitchen scraps such as lemon peels, melon rinds, egg shells, coffee grounds, and any other vegetable waste. Pretend that your compost heap is a lactose-intolerant vegetarian and leave out meat, cheese, milk products, and other animal proteins. They smell rotten and encourage animals to pull your heap apart.

2. Collect garden waste such as last year's leftovers: small twigs, grass clippings, autumn leaves, and weeds. Some say that you should avoid weeds that have gone to seed, but I often forget and therefore I have plenty of weed seeds in my compost. This means that I can't use it on top of the soil without broadcasting weeds that I then have to remove, so I bury my compost in the planting hole where it does the most good, and I don't have to worry.

3. Throw everything in a pile, and when it reaches six to eight inches high, add one or two inches of soil you've dug up from nearby. The soil contains good bacteria that will eat the organic material and break it down.

That's it. As you collect more stuff, add more soil in the same proportion. If you are ambitious, you can turn the pile with a pitchfork, but I don't bother. When I need compost, I push aside some of the stuff at one end and dig underneath. There I find rich brown earth. Well, okay, sometimes it hasn't all broken down completely, so I just chop at the larger bits with my spade and use it all anyway. I find that the pieces of organic material, twigs or corn cobs or whatever, actually help to aerate my heavy clay soil. It breaks down eventually in the planting hole anyway.

HOW TO USE COMPOST

I use it whenever I plant anything. I put it in the bottom of every planting hole, and add a shovelful of compost for every shovelful of earth as I backfill the hole. I throw a layer under bulbs at planting time. When I'm replanting and dividing overgrown clumps, I add a shovelful to the hole for each baby perennial. Sifted, compost becomes humus for flowerpots and window boxes. In real life, I don't use it for that purpose. I could sift the compost through a screen, but who has time? I use commercial potting soil, like everybody else. Compost is an excellent side dressing to spread around shrubs and perennials in spring, but I don't use it that way because mine is so full of seeds. I use wood-chip mulch instead.

"Mulch" is an ugly word for a lovely thing. "Mulch" sounds unattractive and off-putting, like "thrips" or "canker," certainly nothing I'd want to spread near an expensive Aurelian lily. I'm sure more people would use the stuff if it had a French name. So instead of "mulch," from now on I will use the word *mulché!* (pronounced mool-shay), when referring to the organic material I put around my plants. And it will always be followed by an exclamation mark to add excitement.

My favorite *mulché!* is wood chips, which I obtain for free in my local municipal recycling center, or the *centre pour recyclemente,* a location formerly known as the town dump.

There must be money in recycling, because our *centre* is very upscale. It is neater and cleaner than a lot of the streets around town and it is a model of efficiency. This complex of buildings and storage areas has ambience. A large warehouse receives cardboard boxes, newspapers, and furniture. Nearby, a subterranean bin is filled with metal items like dismembered machine parts, refrigerator shelves, brackets, widgets, bicycles, and giant screws. They look interesting all piled together, like modern sculpture. (This observation is either a tip of the hat to the recycling center or a punch in the eye to modern art.)

There are large, clean metal bins filled with glass sorted by color—brown, green, and crystal. You get to throw yours and smash them, which is fun. Plastic bottles are flattened and bundled in neat ten-foot cubes. But for me, the most useful recycled items are the trees. Highway, park, and private tree prunings and removals are brought there to a giant chipper-shredder. The trees and branches go in one end, and at the other is a neatly stacked, ten-foot-high, cone-shaped pile glistening in the sun. There it rises, in beautiful tones of sepia, russet, and raw umber—my obscure object of desire, *le mulché!*

It is yours for the asking, but you must *ask,* or else! You must receive permission from the man who runs the place, "*Monsieur le Général Cliff.*" As you might expect from the master of a dump as neat and clean as this one, *Monsieur le Général Cliff* is something of an anal personality and consequently a control freak. He loves his work. Formerly a corporal in the quartermasters corps in the army before being discharged for mental reasons, he has finally found his *niche* in life, his true *métier.*

Nobody throws a bottle, drops off an auto battery, or discards a fiberglass awning without his say-so. If it's the wrong plastic, it's out. He has been known to refuse refuse if it doesn't measure up to his strict specifications.

And nothing gets taken away without his permission, either. If he catches you sneaking *mulché!,* you are out! But he gives his permission readily as long as the rituals are observed.

We pull up to the heart of the recycling center, the covered newspaper and cardboard area. Cliff is seated on a 1950s-style metal kitchen chair with pearlized black plastic upholstery, no doubt an *objet trouvée.*

Walter gets out of the car before saying good morning, because Cliff won't talk to people in cars. He takes three steps forward, waves, and says hi.

"Are you talking to me, Private?" Cliff begins, setting the tone.

"Morning, sir, how ya doing?" Walter asks, and smiles in his friendliest, most non-threatening way.

"Excellent, Private. We just installed a new metal compactor." He indicates it with his close-cropped head. "We're expanding all the time."

"That's wonderful. Say, is it all right if we take some of that shredded wood over there?"

"What did you say?"

"Wood chips, sir."

"That's better. Which pile, Private?"

"That one." Walter points to a perfect cone across the way. "Sir."

"Can't use that one."

Walter doesn't argue with a man who calls perfect strangers "Private." "Okay, what about that one?" Walter indicates the one nearest the giant chipper-shredder. "Sir."

"What do you want it for?"

Explosives, I'm thinking. But Walter nods in my direction and says, "The little woman wants it for her garden."

"Hmm. All right, Private."

Hurriedly, Walter shovels the *mulché!* while I hold the bag open. When I get it home the precious stuff gets put around and under my favorite shrubs, and between major clumps of perennials. It takes at least a season for the wood to break down, depending on the size of the chips and how thickly I have applied it. Although I have read that *mulché!* can be applied as much as six inches thick, I don't do that in practice. I never have enough of it, so I usually spread it from two to four inches high. Yes, it turns into compost in one season.

Lately, I've heard negative comments about getting wood chips from the recycling center. One person told me that you have to add fungicide and pesticide to the stuff or you will be giving yourself pests, diseases, and weeds for free along with the wood. Somebody else complained that it was full of debris from the roadsides and highways. I have not had any problems with it, and I've been using it for three years, but if you are worried about that kind of thing, by all means, go out and buy commercial wood chip *mulché!*

OTHER MULCHÉS!

Straw: Ruth Stout was one of the pioneers of organic gardening. (Incidentally, she was also the sister of Rex Stout, creator of detective Nero Wolfe, one of the great fictional indoor gardeners of all time.) In 1971, when she was well into her eighties, she wrote the revolutionary *No-Work Garden Book* (Emmaus, Pa.: Rodale Press, 1971), which advocated *mulchéing!* instead of digging, not only to help save other gardeners work but to add fertility to the soil. She contended that a nice, thick, eight-inch layer of straw, added once each year to the vegetable garden, would save hours, perhaps years, of weeding, watering, rototilling, and digging, as well as money spent on fertilizers, herbicides, and pesticides.

She had done this in her own garden and, after a couple of years, the earth under the straw had become rich humus, full of earthworms. To plant, all she did was pull back the straw. Her vegetables stayed high and dry without staking because the straw kept them off the damp earth. And because the soil was constantly enriched, her yields were so large she only had to use half of the land to get the same amount of crop.

I have used a version of her straw *mulché!* method, but because large quantities of straw are not available to me, I used the newspapers covered with wood chips. It worked just as she said it would—the earth stayed moist, fertility increased, and the only weeding I had to do was incidental around the edges.

Leaves: This is nature's *mulché!* I'm one of those people who gratefully accepts autumn leaves from my neighbors. I take the whole pile and blanket my veggie garden. In spring, I rake up what's left without being too neat about it and throw it onto the compost heap. Leftover leaves get incorporated into the soil at planting time or thrown on top of the newspaper *mulché!* I spread around the tomato plants. I like to dig a trench in the vegetable patch, throw in some potatoes that I have cut into pieces, each one containing a sprouting eye, then dump a big pile of leaves on top of them, burying the potato pieces underneath. As the summer wears on and the potato leaves grow taller, I add a few shovelfuls of soil on top. In fall, I dig up the fresh young potatoes and eat them.

Some people chop up their leaves by running the lawn mower over them, which turns them into a combination of *mulché!* and compost. These leaf pieces work even better when used in a mixture with grass clippings, because grass clipping alone get very hot as they break down, sometimes killing the plant and causing the gardener to break down. Compared to other *mulchés!,* the leaf-grass clipping combination biodegrades very quickly.

Sawdust: Good if you live near a sawmill, and it's handy, but sawdust *mulché!* can steal nitrogen from the plants as it breaks down, causing them to turn yellow and die.

When you first start using sawdust, you may have to add a fertilizer containing nitrate of soda, which supplies an instant dose, just to the get the process started. Once the sawdust begins to break down, however, it creates its own nitrogen, just like any other composted material. Organic sources of extra nitrogen are dried blood, bonemeal, and urea. Please note that sawdust made from pine boards will be acidic, just like pine needles. Also, never use sawdust from pressure-treated wood. It contains arsenic. Why do you think the bugs won't eat it?

Black plastic: Is it pretty? Does it biodegrade? Can you eat it? If the answer to any of these questions is no, don't use it. I don't use it.

Weed-barrier mats: Environmentally sound, they are made of geotextile fabric that admits air and water but shades out weeds. It works well in vegetable gardens where appearance is not important, since it looks like some kind of industrial sheeting. Frankly, I think appearance is always important. The manufacturer claims that it will last for three to five years, or much longer if used under other *mulché!* Certainly wood-chip *mulché!* could be used to hide the matting, whose long-term weed-suppressing quality would be useful under shrubs and other places where it's hard to mow. It's not cheap. A strip twenty-four feet long and a yard wide costs from $13 to $20, depending on the thickness of the matting.

Brown cardboard boxes: They're free and they serve the same purpose as weed-barrier mats. They take almost as long to break down, and they're almost as homely.

Rotted cow, horse, sheep manure: Good if you can find it. Better if you can stand it. Best and longest lasting when used with other *mulchés!* such as wood chips or straw.

Coconut fiber, cocoa shells: These are beautiful and expensive unless you live in a southern area where they are plentiful. Cocoa shells are dark brown, and when you first water them, they smell pleasantly like chocolate. Both look a lot like good earth, minus weeds.

HOW TO USE *MULCHÉ!*

I spread *mulché!* from two to four inches thick for reasons already mentioned. I never put the *mulché!* right up against the stem or trunk of the plant because I want to leave a space for air and to prevent the fungus and bacteria that is turning the *mulché!* into delicious compost from doing the same to the plant.

Depending on how often I can get Walter to drive me to the recycling center, I either spread the *mulché!* over the entire garden in late spring, when all the plants have emerged and the soil has warmed up, or, if I am short, and I am, I use it just around selected plants, leaving the areas in between open to allow annuals and biennials to re-seed themselves. Needless to say, weeds will also reseed themselves. I pull.

Last spring, I found a way to stretch the *mulché!* and make an instant no-dig flower border in the bargain. It was an act of horticultural daring, a unique invention that I had never heard of anyone ever attempting before.

My intention was to enlarge the hot-color flower border behind the front fence by about two feet because I wanted to try some of the "Inca Jewels" sunflowers I had seen featured in the Shepherd's Seeds catalog. They came in bright yellow, maroon-banded gold, orange, burgundy, and bronze. They grew from five to eight feet tall and I liked the idea of their large but not grotesquely huge proportions.

To add two more feet to the width of a twelve-foot-long border meant hard work. I would have to spend an entire afternoon digging up the grass, shaking it out, and double digging the area underneath. I didn't have the time. Walter and I had a neighbor's cocktail party to go to that afternoon.

Having used newspaper *mulché!* for the shrub border and the veggie garden, I knew that it was well able to smother what was underneath, so the first thing I did was to spread newspapers five sheets thick over the grass. This looked terrible. If I left it like this, I knew we'd never get asked to another neighborhood cocktail party again. Luckily, I had a black trash bag of wood chip *mulché!* lying around, so I spread that over the newspaper until you couldn't see even a little corner of it sticking out at the edges.

Normally, I would have waited a whole season for the grass to die, break down, and turn into compost, but it was spring and I wanted to plant immediately.

It was then I committed the daring act. I went into the house to get a pair of scissors, my hand trembling with all the excitement of an explorer discovering a new world.

I brushed aside a few wood chips and cut crosses into the newspaper at one-foot intervals. Pulling back the newspaper, I dug out a large plug of the grass about the size and depth of a medium flowerpot, filled it with compost, then replaced most of the newspaper, leaving a small opening into which I planted the sunflower seeds. I watered well and walked away.

You bet it worked! The sunflowers came up like sunshine and never looked back. By this spring, the area under the newspaper has turned into good soil, along with the *mulché!* This spring I will *remulché!* and replant with something else. I have new plans for the hot-color border. The sunflowers were very nice, but two other gardens on the block also had sunflowers and I don't want to use a plant that's trendy. Instead, last fall, I bought a couple of butterfly bushes (*Buddleia Davidii* 'Black Knight'). They grow to about seven feet and have very dark purple flowers that look like small lilac panicles. In fact, sometimes the butterfly bush is called the summer lilac. To set off the deep purple delicate blooms of the shrubs, I've ordered some seeds of Mexican sunflower (*Tithonia rotundifolia*). This tall, bushy variety has daisy-like flowers on six-foot plants that resemble sunflowers, but are bright orange-red instead of yellow. I think orange-red nasturtiums and plum tomatoes growing on the fence would look good with this late summer combo, don't you?

INSTANT MULCHÉ!

After a discussion of the importance of compost and a description of different types of *mulché!*, I must confess my private shame. As I walk around the garden, clipping dead flowers, straightening stems, pulling weeds, I'm too lazy to bring the garden debris back to the compost heap. Every time I have a bunch of wilting weeds in my hand, their little stems dangling pathetically in the warm summer breeze, I twist them into a tight bundle, place them around the base of a nearby plant, and leave them to rot. Nearby leaves, twigs, and grass clippings get similar treatment.

To prevent the garden from looking messier than even I can tolerate, I have developed a couple of tricks. I hide the bundles of weeds behind plants or underneath leaves that shade the ground, like hostas or daylilies. I try to place them in neat little circles around the shrubs. I figure anyone glancing casually at the garden is looking at the flowers, not the little bundles of weedy *mulché!*

The weeds turn brown in a day, and I know that all of us—the leaves, the twigs, the grass clippings, and the gardener—will become earth again in no time. The simple observable fact is that every living thing is *mulché!* and *mulché!* turns into compost by the law of nature. So unless I have a lot of plant material at one time, like during spring cleanup, I expend absolutely no effort shlepping weeds, stems, and clippings in the wheelbarrow and then bringing it back months later as compost. I just keep adding green material right on top.

A lot of people think that a garden with plenty of brown earth showing is the ideal. I admit that there is an aesthetic pleasure in neatness. It's easier to see each object if there is not a lot of irrelevant stuff in the way.

As gardening style, neatness was developed in ancient times mostly due to the fact that there were large numbers of slaves or servants who worked for peanuts. Like large lawns, clipped spotless gardens historically meant that the owner was aristocratic enough to have troops of poor schlemiels picking up twigs for subsistence.

To the mercantile classes of Europe, neatness in the garden became even more important. More specifically, to the English Victorian middle class whose style had such a pervasive influence on our own, a high degree of orderliness became a sign of respectability, like a clean linoleum floor. The fact that there were no stray leaves, twigs, etc., on the lawn or in the flower bed meant that the homeowner was morally upright.

Neatness in the garden was a sign of dominion over chaotic nature and therefore over natural impulses. To be "refined" was the ideal, but to reach it, one had to control or eliminate as much of the "natural" as possible, including sex, illness, childbirth, nose blowing, wind passing, anger, etc. How did they stand it? The only natural function that was permitted was death, which must have come as a welcome relief since life was so boring!

Even today, we all see gardens with neatly turned earth, without a speck of debris, with all the flowers standing in neat rows. The metaphor being touted here is that the higher degree of control over nature the gardener has, the more he is able to control sin, or "wildness." Of course, this is the very ideal that the "wild," "natural" gardeners are rebelling against.

I think it's time to abandon the aesthetic of twigless perfection. Who has the time? Who has the servants? Who cares about sin in the front yard? But most important, we now understand that earth is not endlessly replaceable. If you are growing plants, you must put back what you are taking out, or the soil will eventually be depleted. As any Oklahoman from the dust bowl will tell you, bare earth is doomed earth.

More beautiful to my eyes than a perfect garden without a stray twig, or a "natural" garden without a mistress, is a garden with rich living earth, covered with a large quantity of organic material.

THE DAY I FELL OFF THE CHEMICAL WAGON

The worst insect infestation I ever had occurred a few years ago. A battalion of flea beetles moved in on my sweet autumn clematis (*Clematis terniflora*). The leaves became whitened as though sucked dry and many of them fell off altogether. It was depressing because the vine was large, twenty feet tall, and covered a flagpole. I hauled out the ladder and spritzed the whole thing with soapy water, hoping to wash off the insects and their eggs the way I would do with aphids.

All I got was clean flea beetles.

Desperate, I actually went out and bought rotenone. I repeat: I ACTUALLY WENT OUT AND BOUGHT ROTENONE. It is not considered a particularly dangerous pesticide, but it cost FOURTEEN bucks! I hated doing it.

I applied it wearing rubber gloves, radiation overalls, and an undersea diving helmet, as per package directions, and yes, it worked. All the flea beetles died.

The following season they were back. I had no desire to start mixing chemicals in a spacesuit and spraying that twenty-foot vine again. I decided to ignore them. If anyone asked why the leaves on my beautiful autumn-blooming clematis vine looked so peculiar, I told them to shut up. Just because you are a gardener doesn't mean you have to be nice.

HOW TO AVOID USING PESTICIDES AND HERBICIDES

I find that if the garden is generally healthy, with plenty of sunlight, fresh air, and organic material, diseases are minimal, and pests are eaten by predators, so there are only a few of them. Problems with fungus and diseases are more likely to occur when the garden is stressed by too much or too little rain, poor soil, or the use of too much chemical fertilizer that throws everything out of balance.

Here's what I do to keep my garden healthy:

1. Fungus diseases are usually caused by too much rain over a two-to-three-week period. They are rarely fatal, but my cure is to increase air circulation and sunlight to the plant. Pull nearby weeds to avoid overcrowding. If the patient is being shaded by a desirable neighbor, I move the neighbor or the victim, whichever is easier. At fall cleanup time I discard the previous season's leaves. Fungus often lives in the leaf litter, so I don't put infected leaves in the compost but throw them in the garbage to be taken away.

2. Wilting usually means the plant needs water, or that it is transpiring faster than it can replace fluid. The latter is a common problem with new transplants or seedlings. The answer is to shade the plant from the sun temporarily. To make a natural-looking awning, I cut a spare branch from a nearby tree or shrub and stick it in the ground between the patient and the sun like a beach umbrella. In a few hours, the leaves on the cut branch will wither, but that is usually all the time the transplant needs to recover. (I hope it is common knowledge that a deep soaking once a week is better than a little sprinkling every day.)

3. Virus diseases make the plant look twisted or distorted, the leaves mottled, and the flowers discolored. In general, if the plant starts to get black, brown, sticky, powdery gray, or anything other than healthy green, I simply cut out the bad part. In extreme cases, I cut the whole patient back to the ground. If the virus or other disease comes back or seems to be spreading, I pull out all the infected plants and throw them in the garbage. I also discard any leaves that may have fallen on the ground around them.

4. Bugs: Soft-green insects such as aphids and green worms will be killed by a spray of dishwashing liquid and water. I grab Japanese beetles between my thumb and forefinger and squeeze them to death. Sometimes I drop them in a can of dishwashing liquid and water and drown them.

That's all I do to combat bugs. A healthy plant will recover from being munched on. An unhealthy plant will die. If a plant is repeatedly attacked by insects so that it looks terrible all the time, I assume it is not one that grows easily in my garden and I grow something else.

My secret is to have a great variety of plants, so if a couple of them disappoint me, I still have a beautiful garden.

The next year, the vine recovered and the flea beetles were gone. I don't know why. I think the birds ate them.

Soon after that, I found some potato beetles on my potato plants. I rationalized instead of sprayed. How many potatoes can we eat, anyway? Potatoes are fattening. Oh yes, they are. With butter they are. When I wanted potatoes that year I bought them.

Pest Control

The best kinds of pest control are those that don't affect anything except the particular pest you have to get rid of. Many of these are available in organic gardening catalogs and well-stocked garden centers. I like those apple maggot traps for fruit trees. There are also coddling moth and peach tree borer traps that release sex pheromones, seducing the moths into the trap instead of your fruit. Like the sex traps used for Japanese beetles, these should be placed to lure the insects away from your garden. Sex traps are a good substitute for sprays. Not only do the targeted insects die, they die happy.

Another terrific weapon you can buy is bacillus thuringiensis. It's a poison residue of bacteria that only affects the larvae of certain destructive insects, such as fungus gnats, tomato horn worms, tent caterpillars, and other bugs who eat like horses.

Beneficial nematodes kill grubs of Japanese beetles, cutworms, root weevils, fungus gnats, cabbage-root maggots, and other pests while they are in the larvae stage.

A bat house in a woody area will encourage those physically unattractive but voracious eaters of mosquitoes.

Gypsy moths can't get past a sticky barrier when it is affixed to the trunk of the tree. These are also available.

A tin can half-filled with beer and sunk with its lip at soil level will attract and drown slugs. Once again, they die happy, or at least having forgotten their troubles.

I can't say I never use commercial fertilizers, but I don't use them much. The only fertilizer I use is bulb food, which is basically bonemeal and the treated sewage sludge of Dutch people. Once every two or three years, I have been known to throw some 5-10-5 around. Other than that, I use only compost and *mulché!*

A *mulchéed!* garden is a beautiful garden, full of worms and healthy plants, with a cosmos of life in every square foot. We have all seen those nature shows that take the camera down to ground level and tell us about the sex lives of bugs. It's quite dramatic and at least as interesting as those talk shows about the sex lives of dysfunctional humans. (I want those bugs in my garden a lot more than I want those dysfunctional humans in my neighborhood.) Now imagine all those small creatures on your television screen—a male beetle doing a charming mating dance that makes the female's antennae twitter with passion. Right next to them is a worm couple, head to tail with each other, trying to decide which is the boy and which is the girl. Over yonder are some ants altruistically bringing a seed back to the nest for the children to eat. Suddenly, a gigantic human hand comes into the shot spraying poison onto the earth, killing everything in sight! That is exactly what we are doing when we use herbicides and pesticides.

Many pesticides kill garden-friendly bugs such as bees, ladybugs, and worms along with what we consider destructive insects. Poisonous chemicals are dangerous for pets and children, and they don't do the gardener any good, either. The most repulsive part about using them is not so much that they get on the plants, it's that they get on you. No matter how careful you are, you are bound to get a bit on your skin, or breathe it in while you spray, or brush up against treated plants in the course of gardening.

I know we are told by the manufacturers that the chemicals for home gardens are safe. Oh yeah? They are safe if you don't go near them. Have you read the warnings on the back of a container of pesticide or herbicide? I wouldn't want to sprinkle the stuff on my eggs in the morning. And even if one chemical is safe when used as directed, there are so many different ones, how safe are they all together? What happens when they all get into the ground water? How long do they take to break down? Can they give my grandchildren birth defects? Frankly, I don't know the answer to these questions, and I don't want to be the one to find out.

Agricultural workers have to risk their health to make a living, but I don't. I am a home gardener, not a farmer who depends on one giant commercial agro-maxi-crop for my livelihood.

WEEDING THE GARDEN

Weeding the traditional way is a fool's game, one devised by all those rich people with large staffs of lowly servants.

When I was a kid, current wisdom said you had to pull every weed out by the roots or it would instantly spring back to life like Bela Lugosi from a shallow grave. Since then, I have learned a few other methods. The disadvantage in pulling out the whole plant is that you will expose new earth, which is full of weed seeds just waiting to germinate. If you grab the weed and pull the whole thing out, it's not bad, but there is an intelligent, creative, lazy alternative. Simply cut off the weed at ground level. By removing the leaves, you starve the weed to death. After all, a leafless plant can't produce food. Yes of course the weed will send up new leaves in a panic as quickly as it can, but by the time you have knocked the leaves off a couple of times, most plants give up, especially if the area is then smothered with *mulché!*

Weeding is hardest on the knees. So sit. If you can't reach someplace because it's too far back, leave it alone. So what? Most people only notice if the garden is neat along the edge anyway.

Because I am blessed with short, heavy legs, a heritage from my Polish peasant ancestors, no doubt, I am one of those women who can weed by bending at the hip in the "reach down, touch your toes" position. I have given it a poetic Japanese haiku name, "Full Moon over the Blossoms," and I find it very comfortable. I can weed like that for hours. It only hurts in early spring, before my legs get used to it.

One year, I weeded for twelve hours on the first day of spring. My charley horse was so bad I went to the doctor, who prescribed Norgesic, a well-known muscle relaxer. It made me languid, taking away my pain along with all my anxieties, frustrations, and low self-esteem. It was so terrific, I inquired about getting more. I found out it was highly addictive and, as a result, it was a popular illegal recreational drug. I realized that I should be as careful of the chemicals I dose myself with as those that I use in the garden. Since then, I take a couple of aspirin and, favoring my aches, walk around stiff-legged for a few days each spring looking like a short-legged Rockette doing the goose step.

HOW TO DIG A HOLE

The most frequently injured body part in gardening is not the legs but the lower back, done in by digging incorrectly. We all must dig sometime, if only to make a hole for a tree or shrub. All right. But you can avoid injury by using the right digging tool and knowing the right dance steps.

For digging a hole, use a spade instead of a shovel. There is a big difference between them. A shovel looks like a giant spoon with a rounded bowl and a long handle. A spade has a short handle and a flat, sharp blade that cuts into the earth like a knife through butter.

There is some debate about the importance of the spade you use. I don't think the expensive digging spades are necessarily the best, unlike clippers and other cutting tools where there are big differences between cheap ones and Swiss ones. The length of the handle in relation to your body is more important. My friend Bobbie has an odd one she ordered years ago from the Smith & Hawken catalog. It has a long slender blade with a slightly rounded edge. She swears by the blade, but I think the real reason she loves it so much is its handle length. It is a little shorter than normal, and so is Bobbie.

Good digging is a lot like dancing. Take your spade and place it straight up over the spot you want to dig. Now gracefully hop on it. You may bunny hop with both feet at once, or place one foot on the spade first and stomp with the other, more like a polka. In either case, let your weight do the work of cutting through the sod. Rock the blade side to side, left to right, cha cha cha. When the blade is about halfway through the earth, get off. Pull the handle toward you like a tango partner. Beautiful.

Then lift the dirt and place it behind you. *Never place the dirt in front of you.* That way lies the chiropractor's office. When you put the weight in front, you are bending and using your back muscles; when you put the weight behind, you're using your arm and stomach muscles. (Sore arm and stomach muscles don't leave you crippled for weeks!)

Repeat until the hole is dug or the music stops.

I have an interesting little shrub that was in my garden when I bought the house. It is a shrub clematis, a version of the famous vine with attractive panicles of small tasteful white flowers. Until now, I had never seen it in anyone else's garden, a fact of which I was secretly proud. The problem with the plant, however, is that it flops over as soon as the flowers open. I don't mean the flowers droop like daisies after a rain, no, the whole plant falls over on its neighbors like an upside-down umbrella. It's terrible.

Last summer in England, I was strolling past the famous long border with Christopher Lloyd, trying desperately to be interesting, when I saw my shrub clematis, blooming right in the middle of the long border at Great Dixter!

Great Scott! It was standing up!

"Whoa, Mr. Lloyd!" I exclaimed, interrupting something he was saying. "Isn't that a shrub clematis?"

"Yes, it's called *Clematis recta,*" he replied mildly, considering my excitement.

"*Recta?* Doesn't that mean 'erect'?" I asked, raising my eyebrows and smiling suggestively.

A brief glimmer flickered in his eye. Was he enjoying the double entendre? "Yes, it does mean erect, which is ironic, because the plant flops over dramatically as soon as it starts blooming."

Didn't I know it! "But your clematis is as erect as anything I'd ever want to see."

"Thank you," he said modestly. Was he laughing? Hard to tell. "It's the pea sticks."

I looked more closely. Sure enough, the whole plant was underpinned with pea sticks, twiggy tree branches that had been placed around the plant to support the weak stems.

"You know, sir, mine flops, too. So how did it come to be called *recta?*"

"Perhaps botanists have a sense of humor."

I'd swear that they do.

Don't Plant Magenta Next to Taxicab Yellow!

BOY, I HATE that combination. All over the countryside in late summer, I see bright yellow black-eyed susans growing next to dull purpley-pink phlox, and it makes me sick. Magenta *Rosa rugosa* next to orange tiger lilies also make me shudder. After going to all the effort of planting a garden, sweating over the earth, weeding the beds, why put clashing colors next to each other? I don't understand it. I mentioned my aversion once on morning television, and the hostess said to me, "What's wrong with that combination? You see it in nature all the time!"

"You don't have to do everything nature says, Kathie Lee," I replied. "If I did everything nature said, I'd have twelve children by now!"

"I'd have a hundred!" she retorted, topping me, at least in numbers.

It has been my experience that the average person looking at a pretty flower garden isn't concerned whether the colors clash. Most people find it pleasing enough if there are a lot of flowers. There is nothing wrong with this approach. A healthy garden full of many colors has a lovely, unself-conscious charm. But when you compare it to a garden made by a master of color, may I say it pales?

168

Getting the colors right is one of the most satisfying aspects of gardening, and for me it is the most fun. I enjoy it so much that I purposely left writing this chapter until last as a reward for finishing the rest of the book.

A garden room is like a room in the house, and will look better if the curtains match the carpet and the couch doesn't clash with the wallpaper, metaphorically speaking. Having a color scheme in mind limits the choice of plant material, which is a big help when you're planning a new garden, and gives you a bit of discipline when you go to the garden center. You will think twice about buying that annual red salvia just because it's on sale. I'd think twice about it anyway. It is a peculiar shade of tomato red that clashes with just about everything, even tomatoes. It's always just a little "off," horrible next to pink, disgusting near purple, and cheesy next to yellow of any shade. Can you tell I don't like it?

THE ART OF COLOR

Here are ten points about color from the masters, including my personal observations. Remember, these are points of reference, not hard-and-fast rules. Talented people can make anything look fabulous, but these come in very handy for we lesser mortals:

1. For maximum impact, use colors that are opposite each other on the color wheel (see page 171). In other words, blue with orange (think of Van Gogh's painting of blue irises), red with green (Christmas), and yellow with purple (my old school colors).

2. When combining two colors, it is more interesting if they are in unequal proportion to each other. Combinations of equal numbers—six yellow marigolds next to six purple petunias—look boring. A proportion of three to one (3:1) is much more interesting. Imagine nine yellow marigolds and three purple petunias or, if you prefer, nine purple petunias and three yellow marigolds. The dominant color makes the statement, the submissive color points to the first by contrast. This relationship has intrinsic drama, as you may imagine.

3. Use one or two main colors for a given area of the garden, then add one or two others to contrast. For example, in my front garden, the main colors are warm yellows and dark reds. To this odd, strong combination, I add a touch of purple or orange and a lot of neutrals.

4. Green is the great garden neutral, but true blue, white, and cream-colored flowers, as well as gray-leaved plants, are also neutrals and will enhance *any* color combination.

5. In my experience, you can't go wrong if you put cool colors like rose-pink and purple together, and hot colors like yellow, red, and orange, together. Everything goes with the neutrals.

6. When mixing many colors all together, it helps if they are of they same intensity. Pale shades of red, yellow, purple, and orange become pink, primrose, lavender, and apricot, which never fight with one another. Bright red, yellow, purple, and orange of equal intensity are at least a match for one another.

7. Light and dark tones of all one color are pretty reliable. Pink to red, apricot to deep copper, cream to gold, and lavender to royal purple work beautifully.

8. Avoid mixing pastels and intense colors that are *nearly opposite* each other on the color wheel. This produces the kinds of color combinations you see in 1970s clothing, usually in polyester. For example, hot peach and purple, pale turquoise and cardinal red, or pale blue and tomato red. We are saved from making these combinations in the garden since many of these colors thankfully do not exist in nature. When they do, the results can only be described as revolting. This is the cause of my repulsion by that combination of taxicab-yellow black-eyed susan vs. lavender phlox.

9. Bright or light colors are best if you intend to see the garden from a distance. They show up against the pervading green and brown of the rest of nature the

way those red or yellow numbers did on the color blindness tests we took in school. The conspicuous quality of these colors is the reason "Yield Right of Way" traffic signs used to be yellow and "Stop" signs bright red. (Since the introduction of reflective materials, however, the bright colors of many street signs have yielded right-of-way to tasteful green.)

10. Cool or deep colors are most easily seen up close but are lost from across the yard. From a distance, colors in the blue to purple range recede into the blue yonder. That doesn't mean we shouldn't grow varieties that feature these colors. Of course not. But they are best used as delightful or dramatic contrast to the lighter, brighter colors.

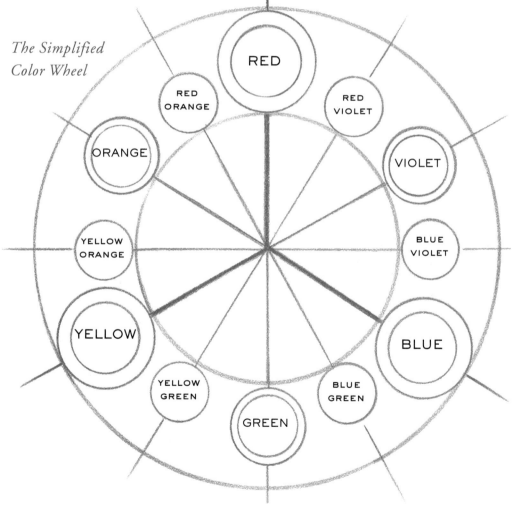

The Simplified Color Wheel

RED

RED ORANGE

RED VIOLET

ORANGE

VIOLET

YELLOW ORANGE

BLUE VIOLET

YELLOW

BLUE

YELLOW GREEN

BLUE GREEN

GREEN

These ten points are guidelines to help you avoid making errors, but if you find you have inadvertently made a color combination that annoys you, offends you, or positively socks you in the eye every time you go by, don't despair. You can always move the plant, and until then, do what I do: cut off all the offending flowers and put them in a vase in the house.

COLOR GARDENS

In the early part of the twentieth century, it was fashionable to make single-color gardens. The English writer Vita Sackville-West popularized the one-color trend at her estate, Sissinghurst. In some of her gardens, she used colors refined to the point of decadence. She had a purple border. Her all-white garden contained only plants with white flowers and gray leaves. As we know, many plants with gray leaves, like wormwood (*Artemisia latiloba*) and lamb's ears (*Stachys lanata*), have yellow or magenta flowers, which had to be assiduously chopped off to maintain the theme.

She also had a garden of mauve, a color so subtle and ephemeral, it's dull. You can't get more elegant than that.

Vita herself was refined to the point of decadence. Color ruled her very passions. When she had an extramarital affair, it was with a woman named Violet, and I doubt that she allowed Violet into the white garden.

Nowadays, single-color gardens are considered corny, the obsessive hobbies of wealthy women with artistic pretensions and compulsive personalities. But I love the idea. When starting a garden, a single color is a most delightful way to find a unifying theme, and there is no law that says you have to keep it one color forever.

In the hopes that it will inspire you, and because it is fun to plan imaginary gardens, let's pretend we are making single-color rooms and look at the possibilities that are presented. Remember that the particular color is just a starting point, a word to add to the "theme," as Mary Keen would say. As we go along, I will feel free to include a discussion of each color in relation to others. I will also feel free to add relevant stories, impertinent remarks, and pointless digressions, as usual.

To be honest, I've never seen a white garden in person unless you count the garden of my friend Don, who is color-blind. He grows four thousand white daffodils in his woodland in early spring. It's lovely.

An all-white-flowered garden is visually interesting not by its contrasts of color, but by changes in light, shadow, and form. Without the element of color, which has a high entertainment value all by itself, form and structure become more important. So for our garden, the overall shape of the plants must be well defined. A rounded, white-flowered hydrangea in front of a tall clump of white-plumed pampas grass is a dramatic contrast of forms. We'll repeat this combination around the perimeter of the garden. Now we will plant white-flowered varieties of the common garden plants. A lot of small plants with white flowers all jumbled together resemble snow on a TV screen, so we will plant large clumps and drifts of each.

We have a wide variety of plants from which to choose. After all, almost every species has a white version of its flower. Only some yellow flowers have no gene for white. That is why for years the Burpee company offered a ten-thousand-dollar reward to the home gardener who could hybridize a "white" marigold. The one that was finally produced was colorless, all right, all traces of yellow having been bred out of it, but I have one question for the Burpee company: Who wants a white marigold?

We fill our borders with white lilies, white peonies, white delphiniums, alliums, tulips, hyacinths, roses, astilbes, lilies of the valley, carnations, bleeding hearts, irises, and the rest. Fragrant white-flower shrubs like lilac (*Syringa* 'Miss Ellen Willmott') and mock orange (*Philadelphus spp.*) are planted around the perimeter. Their dreamlike white flowers gleam in the twilight as the sun fades at the end of the day.

I'm told that once you are committed to it, a white garden is "colorful" in a subtle, restrained, understated way. After a while, they say, you can discern a whole world of white. And so we can! We can see many shades and textures—from the pale bluc-white of wisteria that grows along the top of the white-columned pergola, the pink-white of apple blossoms trained against the dark green fence, the pure innocent white of daisies falling over the brick paths, the crinkled white tissue paper of poppies, the chalky white of *Nicotiana alata,* the pale ivory velvet of old roses, the yellowing, heavy crème brûlée of sweet autumn clematis. Gray-leaved plants like lamb's ears and artemesia add more paleness to the landscape.

From what I have seen, only the purest of the purists can maintain an all-white garden forever. Even the famous White Flower Farm catalog started out offering only white flowers, but quickly drifted into the colorful flower business. I don't blame them. As a flower lover, color is my business, too.

When I first heard that Vita Sackville-West's white garden at Sissinghurst was not on the itinerary of my television visit to British gardens, I was disappointed. But I felt much better when I was told that another place on my tour, Kiftsgate Court, also had a white garden. It was described as a sunken garden surrounding a fountain in a courtyard. It sounded beautiful, and I couldn't wait to see it.

Kiftsgate Court is a substantial, graceful building in the classical style. It is made of beautiful aged stone and has Corinthian columns across the front. Imagine the New York Public Library as a private house, and you'll get the idea. It is surrounded by the classic English arrangement of garden rooms, of a scale and size equal to the house.

The owner, Anne Chambers, was as lovely and grand as the place. Slender and fair, she's the woman Martha Stewart is trying to imitate. She was so refined and elegant, I felt insecure and inadequate as she began to take me around on the garden tour. With the television camera discreetly right in front of our faces, I felt even more under scrutiny. I was afraid she was seeing me as a bourgeois, ill-bred, vulgar arriviste from Brooklyn—in other words, the real me. Desperate, at first I tried faking a British accent.

"Rally, this gahden is veddy veddy chawming," I complimented her, trying to sound like the mistress of Elsing Hall with the magnificent roses, Shirley Cargill Not from Brooklyn. "Quaht extrawdnerry!"

"What part of New York are you from?" Anne asked.

"Manhattan," I lied.

But she was human, too. Between shots, she confided in me that she was very nervous about being on television! Imagine! My attempts to put her at ease made me forget my own self-consciousness and we had a wonderful time after that.

She first led me to the pride of the place, the famous Kiftsgate rose. This rambler rose is one of the largest single specimens in the world and was named after this estate. As we walked through the gardens, I could only imagine what such a huge plant would look like covered in roses. At last, we turned the corner into the rose garden and there it was!

"Here's the Kiftsgate rose!" Anne exclaimed.

"Where?" All I saw was a mass of green foliage.

"Here!"

"Where?"

"Here!"

It was not in bloom! Not one flower!

There were multiple buds on each stem and Anne said that when it did bloom, it would have tens of thousands of fragrant, old-fashioned, single white flowers, but it had been a cool summer and I was a week early. What a disappointment!

Even out of bloom, the Kiftsgate rose was still quite a tourist attraction. I mentioned in the last chapter that roses grow easily in England. This one climbed ninety feet into an enormous old tree. Ninety feet, I said. Ninety feet is bigger than a house, bigger than a brontosaurus. It was not the sort of rosebush you can prune in an idle afternoon. They maintain it by slashing it back every year when branches at the bottom threaten to block the path of the rose garden, otherwise they leave this prickly dragon alone. Would you want to tangle with a ninety-foot thorn factory?

I examined the giant plant with a more critical eye than I would have if it had been blooming. Anne told me it had originally been discovered in the Himalayas, but to me, it looked suspiciously like that pestilential weed, the *Rosa multiflora,* which strangles the trees along the roadsides in upstate New York. It had similar light green leaves, it had multiple buds on each stem, it had white flowers (supposedly), and it sure had the vigorous growth habit, although I doubted this giant was hardy in upstate New York. I was too polite to suggest to my gracious hostess that her prize attraction looked like a weed in my backyard, so I didn't. Anyway, I was probably wrong about it. Who am I, a bourgeois arriviste from Brooklyn, to judge the pedigree of an aristocratic one-of-a-kind English rose?

The rest of the rose garden consisted of two very deep borders with a straight path running down the middle. The borders contained shrub roses blooming in all the pale to rose madder (magenta) pink shades of the antique varieties. Along the path was a low hedge of the medieval *Rosa mundi*. At the end of the path, there was a modern abstract nude female statue made of weathered green copper. It was a perfect focal point for this abundant rose garden, a long way from plastic gnomes on the lawn, let me tell you.

Anne next showed me a hundred-foot-long garden walk flanked by borders whose main colors were mauve (yes, mauve), rosepink, purple, and cream, softened and harmonized by plants with blue-and-gray leaves. Lovely. Then she showed me her yellow border, which had plenty of yellow flowers, but also big cobalt blue delphiniums, which underlined the point I made earlier about the blue-yellow combo. This lady really knew how to use color. Finally, we turned the corner of a ten-foot hedge into the white garden!

There were the steps leading down to the fountain. There was the fountain. "Here's the white garden!" Anne announced.

"Where? Where?" I searched frantically, my hopes becoming as sunken as the garden. The place was full of pink valerian, purple violas, blue campanulas, yellow roses, blushing poppies, lavender alliums!

"Here!"

"Where?"

"Here!"

"Where?"

"Here!"

"Why is it called the white garden, Anne?" I asked politely.

"It was white in my grandmother's day." How typically British.

"This garden reminds me of the Mae West line, 'I used to be Snow White, but I drifted,' " I offered.

"Yes, ha, ha. Just so. It has drifted, I admit. I've allowed a lot of things to seed themselves, but I like color, don't you?"

"As a matter of fact, Anne, I do. You see, color is my business."

THE BLUE GARDEN

Most of us have a favorite color and, statistically, most people say it is blue. The idea of an all-blue garden is very appealing. Blue-flowered plants have refinement and rarity, two qualities that give them a great deal of social, and therefore horticultural, cachet.

What annoys me about blue flowers is their superior, "more precious than pink" snob appeal. It's not the flowers' fault. In haute horticultural circles, blue flowers are generally considered to be more high-toned and desirable than yellow ones, and don't even mention orange. In other words, you should grow blue flowers in order to command respect from the country club—the same reason many people take up golf.

Of course, there are lots of unpretentious, spiritually advanced gardeners who honestly prefer flowers that are subtle and murmur rather than shout. Blue flowers, like the balloon flower (*Platycodon grandiflorum*), the species delphinium (*Delphinium belladonna*), and many others, add glamour to any color scheme. An area of trees underplanted with sky blue Virginia bluebells (*Mertensia virginica*) is breathtaking in May, as is a slope blanketed with royal blue Siberian squill (*Scilla sibirica*) in March.

I enjoyed a magical garden sighting one afternoon, a couple of years ago, when I glanced into the courtyard of a New York City apartment house and found it filled with hydrangeas in full bloom. Their large, heart-shaped leaves were covered with huge blue pouffes the color of Mel Gibson's eyes. I don't know which was more thrilling, the sight of so many flowers in the middle of the city, or the fact that they were *so* blue!

It would be difficult to make a whole garden of plants with only true blue flowers. For one thing, there aren't that many of them. As we know, most flowers called "blue" in plant catalogs are really lavender or purple-blue. But when it comes to honest blue, cobalt blue, sky blue, true-friend blue without a hint of purple ego, the list is not long. We must content ourselves with a few heroes. As well as those already mentioned, forget-me-nots (*Myosotis sylvatica*), bachelor's button (*Centaurea cyanus*), bugloss (*Anchusa*), flax (*Linum perenne*), morning glory (*Ipomoea tricolor*), and love-in-a-mist (*Nigella damascena*) are among the few common garden plants with true blue flowers.

Gertrude Jekyll, who loved color in gardens as much as the next artistic, obsessive Englishwoman, stated that a blue garden should have some yellow or orange in it. Yellow and orange, she asserted, give the recessive blues a lot of zest and actually improve their "blueness," making even the purpley blues look truer. Using the proportion three to one (3:1), according to point 2 in the guidelines on page 169, we add white to this blue garden, along with some yellow and orange flowers—like daylilies, yellow columbines, orange tulips, yellow dahlias. We now have roughly three blue plants to one yellow, white, or orange of the same size. The hot colors set the blues off by contrast, the way a fat friend makes you look thinner.

You don't usually associate blue flowers with late summer, but there are several azure-flowered shrubs that we must have for our blue garden. The mophead hydrangea (*Hydrangea macrophylla*) that everyone buys for Mother's Day actually blooms in July in New York gardens. Its big round flowers are pink or blue, like the ones I saw in the apartment house courtyard. You get the hydrangeas to turn blue by growing them in acidic soil. There are even more elegant forms of hydrangea flowers, called lace caps, which also come in blue. We can't live without whole drifts of those blue-flowered sub-shrubs, the Russian sage (*Perouskia atriplicifolia*) and the blue mist shrub (*Caryopteris* x *clandonensis*). For height and substance, we plant rose-of-Sharon (*Hibiscus syriacus* 'Bluebird').

For most purposes, true blue is a stunning color when used as an accompaniment to other colors, to bring out their clarity. Blue makes a wonderful sidekick; it is Robin not Batman, Sancho Panza not Don Quixote, Horatio not Hamlet.

Blue defines other colors by elimination. It's as if you were saying: "How do you like this pink? Pink, isn't it? This color is not blue. Look, here is blue, and this is not it." Blue works on behalf of *all* the other colors in this way.

The other universally neutral garden color is green, of course. It is the background against which other colors are viewed and, like blue, defines them. That's why blue-green is such a magical color with which to paint garden furniture. Claude Monet painted his garden structures a bright blue-green, somewhere between aquamarine and turquoise, and he knew what he was doing because he was a famous artist and lived in France.

I felt that aquamarine was a little too Folies-Bergère for my brown Gothic house in upstate New York, so I painted my fences and metal chairs "Essex Green" by Benjamin Moore, which is a very, very dark blue-green.

In England, you might be interested to know, it is currently fashionable in haute hort circles to paint metal garden furniture a color somewhere between navy and royal blue. Anne Chambers painted her iron Victorian garden furniture this color in the "white" garden and it was stunning.

THE RED GARDEN

I don't know why the human eye is so attracted to red. Perhaps it's because we are carnivores and red means fresh meat. Or perhaps it's because healthy lips and excited sexual parts are red. In any case, we love it.

When you think of an all-red garden, you imagine that it would be very bright, even—dare I say it?—vulgar. Like the Christmas edition of a Victoria's Secret catalog, a red garden evokes the swoosh of scarlet chiffon, the caress of carmine velvet, the rustle of red satin.

A red garden sounds hot, hot, hot, but it's not. In fact, when we combine red-flowering plants like poppies with maroon-leafed plants, such as Japanese maples (*Acer japonica*), red basil (*Ocimum basilicum*), and coralbells (*Heuchera americana* 'Palace Purple'), to name a few, a strange thing happens. The reds aren't bright anymore. I would go so far as to say the effect is dark and restful.

We start our red garden by planting three of my favorite shrubs with red flowers, the beauty bush, weigela, which is covered with red trumpets in early summer; the spring-blooming Japanese flowering quince (*Chaenomeles japonica*), which is actually coral; and, of course, the greatest red-flowered shrub of all, the rose. *Rosa floribunda* 'Europeana' is the "reddest" red rose I know. It is a true, lush crimson—I'm talking about crush-my-mouth-with-kisses red—a red to make a vampire hungry. I saw it advertised in a catalog once and they recommended that it be used as a hedge, which sounds about as tasteful as upholstering the inside of the Caddie with red fake fur. Too much.

But one or three bushes look sensational in front of our ten-foot-tall smoke tree (*Cotinus Coggygria* 'Royal Purple'), a shrub with maroon leaves. We place one more as the focal point of a long flower border. We place another one at the opening of a dark evergreen hedge.

Even our vines have red flowers. The common variety of the red trumpet vine (*Campsis radicans*) grows over the pergola as rampantly as a wisteria. The color is a decided orange-red that echoes the color of the old-fashioned potted geraniums on the table underneath. Although we have not used it here, there is also a blue-red trumpet vine called Crimson Trumpet that is available from catalogs. A red-flowered honeysuckle, also called, monotonously, Crimson Trumpet (*Lonicera sempervirens*), drapes the fence. Its blooms are a soft true red, lovelier, though not as fragrant, as the common yellow-and-white Hall's variety. We have combined it with the annual scarlet runner bean vine. If we lived in a warm part of the country, zone eight southward, the bougainvillea would be *the* stunning red flowering vine to plant. It comes in other colors, like pink and cream, but also several shades of red from hot crimson to almost maroon.

Red nasturtiums grow along the path, in front of self-sown red-leaf basil and a taller red-leaf version of love-lies-bleeding (*Amaranthus caudatus*). These set off the true red cardinal lobelia (*Lobelia cardinalis*), named after the bird, I'm sure. Ten-foot red hollyhocks (*Althaea rosea*), tiny coralbells (*Heuchera sanguinea*), the overpowering eight-inch blooms of red Southern Belle hibiscus (*Hibiscus moscheutos*), along with plenty of red daylilies (*Hemerocallis*) in different sizes and shades, Asiatic lilies, bee balm (*Monarda* 'Cambridge Scarlet'), and true red oriental poppies (*Papaver orientale*) make up the flower parade.

After a couple of seasons (or maybe a couple of minutes), it occurs to us to add a few softer colors to our mainly red color scheme, like cream-colored roses or pink dianthus. Gray-leaved plants soften the bright flowers very satisfactorily, so we start collecting artemesia, rue, and yucca with blue-gray leaves to plant in and around the bright flowers.

When used in a border with other colors, a large blob of bright red takes over. You may have noticed this effect in tulip plantings in public parks. There may be four different color stripes in the bed, but you see the red ones first.

In most gardens, a little red goes a long way. I like to use red flowers as a bit of peppery spice in the center of a group of paler plants. For example, a few sprays of coralbells among a drift of white daisies and blue balloon flowers gives them zip.

Bright red is best if you don't make a big deal of it, but use it to emphasize a point of interest, the way red lipstick draws the eye to the face, especially when wearing a beige suit. A pot of red geraniums will draw the eye to a bench, an urn, or the exit. In an otherwise quietly colored garden, red flowers flanking the door tell you where to go.

THE YELLOW GARDEN

Whenever I mention the idea of an all-yellow border, people turn up their nose. Yellow is too bright, too cheerful, too relentlessly perky, they complain. I suspect the real objection is that a yellow garden is too easy in North America. Like Rita Zuchavitzky, the easiest girl in high school: when everyone could have her, nobody wanted her. (No, I was not the easiest girl in high school. I was an intellectual. I was the groupie for the chess team. I used to run around the room yelling, "Mate! Mate!" Not that it did me much good.)

But let me quote Louise Beebe Wilder, one of the most artistic, respected, tony American gardeners of the early twentieth century: "As I have said many times I am not fond of gardens or borders devoted to one colour . . ." (Notice how she spells color with a *u*. Back in the early part of the century, using British spelling was suave, and I'll bet she sounded like Katharine Hepburn when she talked. Nowadays we would call that affected.) ". . . but if ever I were tempted to make one it would be yellow. . . . Not all blue flowers may be safely used in each other's company and but few pinks unless they are of the same scale"—How refined to be offended by clashing pinks!—"but all yellow flowers, like the light of which they are fashioned, blend and combine or flash back at each other with never a jar to the most sensitive eye."* Or the most sensitive stomach.

---

*Louise Beebe Wilder, *Color in My Garden* (New York: Atlantic Monthly Press, 1990).

I don't agree with Madame Louise Beebe Wilder about the blues and pinks. In my experience, pinks or blues almost always look good, with a few exceptions, like orangey pink with a very purply pink, maybe. I think she's absolutely right about the yellows, however.

If a yellow garden was good enough for Madame Beebe Wilder, it's good enough for us. Plants with yellow flowers are plentiful and many are indigenous to North America, so we immediately plant sunflowers, black-eyed susans, and goldenrods to bloom at the end of the summer in our garden.

Yellow looks sensational in the spring as well. Daffodils, crocuses, hyacinths, and tulips all come up in many shades of yellow, not to mention the early-spring bloom-ing winter aconite (*Eranthus* hyemalis), and the magnificent yellow form of the stately, four-foot, pineapple-shaped Crown Imperial (*Fritillaria imperialis* 'Lutea Maxima'). Just to be redundant for the fun of it, we plant primrose-colored tulips to bloom among the primroses.

In summer, growing on the pergola, we have yellow roses, such as the antique Har-rison's Yellow, and the modern climber with the kinky name, Golden Showers.

We mustn't forget to add a member of the pea family, the June-blooming *Thermop-sis mollis,* with the sweetest yellow flowers you can imagine. And we must also include the tall, somewhat phallic foxtail lily (*Eremurus robustus*), and the taller, definitely phallic six-foot, silver-leaved mullein (*Verbascum thapsus*).

In front of the taller perennials, we have daylilies in every shade of yellow imag-inable, from almost white to almost orange. Passing by the gate, we can smell the fragrant yellow Aurelian lilies as they come up right through the orangey-yellow daisies of the threadleaf coreopsis (*Coreopsis verticillata*). And of course there are yellow columbines, irises, and tall yellow hollyhocks growing nearby. We do not hesitate to include daisies and other flowers with yellow centers, like Japanese peonies, with their single row of white petals surrounding a golden mass of stamens and pistils.

Here's a dry spot. Let's add *Achillea* 'Moonglow' and 'Coronation Gold', and some herbs with yellow flowers like tansy.

What about yellow tomatoes on supports? yellow squash yellow cherries?

Our garden is surrounded by small trees with yellow blossoms like the golden chain tree (*Laburnum* x *Watereri*) and a magnificent specimen of magnolia Elizabeth, with pale yellow saucers instead of pink ones, in spring. We also have trees with yellow leaves such as the locust (*Robinia*) or the golden weeping willow (*Salix*). The maple tree we have planted (in the *far* distance!) is a ball of sunshine in October.

Planted along the back fence are spring-blooming shrubs with yellow flowers, such as the forsythia (*Forsythia* x *intermedia*), or the more interesting witch hazel (*Hamamelis*), winter hazel (*Corylopsis glabrescens*), Oregon holly grape (*Mahonia*), and red-vein enkianthus (*Enkianthus campanulatus*), with its delicate bells. In May, we have the spectacular Chinese tree peony (*Paeonia lutea*), with enormous yellow flowers that look as though they are made of crepe paper.

Yellow-leaved shrubs include spirea Goldflame and yellow variegated euonymus (*Euonymus aureo-marginatus*). I would go easy on yellow-leaved plants, frankly. Sometimes it's hard to tell if the yellow leaves are a result of hybridization, imminent death by iron deficiency, or maybe it's autumn.

The only problem with a yellow garden is that all that perky sunshine really is boring without some contrast, as Madame Beebe Wilder has already observed. Following point 1 at the beginning of this chapter (see page 169), we also have plants from the opposite side of the color wheel, purple-blue delphiniums, lavender catnip (*Nepeta mussinii*), blue balloon flower (*Platycodon*), and purple sage (*Salvia superba*) appear at intervals. We have planted them in roughly the proportion of three yellow to one blue or purple-flowering plant as per point 2. Of course, the other neutral flower colors, white and cream, along with plants with gray or bluish leaves, soften and smooth the yellows together "like buttah."

A yellow garden shows up best against a dark house, or against a dark green hedge or fence. Garden furniture and garden structures for a yellow garden would look great in blue, green, blue-green, gray, and brown.

THE GRAY GARDEN

Some people might think a garden composed of plants with gray leaves would be sad or mournful. And they are right. Some old monastery gardens were all gray to remind the monks of the sins of this world and the ashes to which they would soon return. Despite that dreary intent I think a gray garden could also look very sophisticated and chic, especially with modern architecture.

Plants with gray leaves have several good points. Deer hate to eat most of them, they tend to thrive in difficult, arid conditions, their leaves are frequently aromatic and good for making into wreaths and other decorative floral arrangements, and they are beautiful in a ghostly way.

Our gray garden is surrounded by small Russian olive trees (*Elaeagnus angustifolia*), their leaves flashing silver in every passing breeze, and weeping pears (*Pyrus salicifolia* 'Pendula'). Dwarf blue spruce (*Picea pungens*) and slate gray junipers (*Juniperus scopulorum* 'Moonglow') are planted as focal points in the center of each flower bed.

Shrubs include the seven-foot butterfly bush (*Buddleia Davidii*) with blue-gray leaves and mauve-to-blue flowers; the pale, blue-flowered Russian sage (*Perovskia atriplicifolia*); and *Fothergilla* 'Blue Mist', with honey-scented white fuzzball flowers and almost-blue leaves. In warmer zones we can include the twelve-to-eighteen-foot chaste tree (*Vitex agnus-castus*) from southern Europe, with its gray-green foliage and fragrant lavender flowers.

Our flower beds are filled with herbaceous plants with gray, green-gray, and blue-gray leaves, such as pinks (*Dianthus plumarius*) and lamb's ears (*Stachys lanata*), as well as herbs like catnip (*Nepeta Mussinii*), rosemary (*Rosmarinus officinalis*), lavender (*Lavandula*), rue (*Ruta graveolens*), and yarrow (*Achillea millefolium*). We have hostas like Krossa Regal with bluish-green leaves; blue grasses such as fescue (*Festuca glauca*); tall flowering plants such as mullein (*Verbascum thapsus*), an eight-foot beauty with fuzzy, almost white foliage and soft yellow flowers; Scotch thistle (*Onopordum acanthium*), a twisted, sculptural six-foot biennial that looks as if it's covered in frost; and across the way from them, pink-flowered sea holly (*Eryngium maritimum*); the bluish-green, dramatically shaped *Euphorbia Wulfenii*, rose campion (*Lychnis coronaria*), and all the lacy leaf shapes of many varieties of the Artemisia family.

Woolly thyme (*Thymus serpyllum lanuginosus*) grows in the cracks in the gray stone paths. Wall cress (*Arabis albida*), sedum, snow-in-summer (*Cerastium tomentosum*), and *Lamium* 'Beacon Silver' grow along the edges.

A purist like Vita Sackville-West might cut off the flowers for fear of ruining the color scheme—but really! Flower colors, whatever they are, are especially dramatic in such a garden, so we leave the blooms alone. We put a sofa and cocktail table there and hang out at twilight with Walter, sipping cool clear martinis and celebrating the fact that we are not yet ashes.

THE GREEN GARDEN

The nearest thing to a truly green garden I've ever seen was in New Hope, Pennsylvania. It belonged to David Benner, a tall slender college professor with a passion for moss. David's moss garden was in a heavily wooded area. (It's no use even to think of doing a moss garden unless you have an area that is damp and shady and somewhat acidic.)

When he first bought it, his house had a conventional front lawn under trees. To turn it into a moss garden, he cut the grass less than an inch high, added soil acidifier, which would favor the acid-loving moss over the lime-loving grass, and waited. Sure enough, the grass died and the moss thrived.

Eventually, David landscaped his entire property with mosses, ferns, and other shade-loving woodland plants, most of which showed up by themselves as soon as he stopped mowing and provided the right conditions. He now has twenty-five different varieties of moss, some that resemble green felt, some as tall as six inches that look like miniature ferns. He swore he has never introduced any of them; they found their way to his yard all by themselves. He even showed me a rare wildflower he had discovered growing in his moss.

We walked all over the place without discernible harm to the moss, although it's not as durable as grass for high-traffic areas. Then again, grass is not as durable as cement, so what? How often do you give ballroom dancing lessons on the front lawn, anyway?

The secret to keeping a great moss garden is to prevent the autumn leaves from smothering it. Leaves are removed by hand rake in tiny Japanese moss gardens, but that is hardly practical in a large eastern woods maintained by one person. In early fall,

David throws black plastic netting (the kind that is used to keep birds off fruit trees) over the moss and keeps it there while the leaves are falling. When all the trees are bare, he picks up the netting and carts off the leaves. This allows the moss to get light and air all winter.

The moss garden was beautiful and graceful and very romantic, a mantle of green velvet clothing the undulating ground and the rock walls, softening all the angles, making even the stones tender.

The one-color garden is just a starting point for our fantasies. Now let's put a couple of colors together. For example, let's mix the gray garden and the yellow garden in equal parts. Immediately, we have created a visually and psychologically interesting situation. The relentless cheer of all that yellow has been softened and restrained by the grays. Here we have contained the conflict between cheer and gloom, life and death, laughter and forgetting. They balance each other. Now we desire to add another color, one that will reconcile the other two, as per point 3 in the guidelines. We take purple from the other side of the color wheel. Dark purple flowers such as tulips and irises will do for spring. In summer, monkshood, along with several specimens of the seven-foot butterfly bush 'Black Knight', will point up the yellow and gray.

Or what if we do something else entirely and create a rainbow of changing color as the garden season goes on? We begin with a yellow spring garden with its crocuses, tulips, and daffodils, choose yellow-orange azaleas and wallflowers for late spring, red-flowering plants for rose season, purple and lavender flowers such as aconite, phlox, and catnip for summer, those wonderful blue shrubs for late summer, and back to yellow sunflowers for the fall? Of course, some of the plants would overlap, but that would be part of the interest and beauty of it. Anyway, it's fun to sit with a bunch of illustrated catalogs and dream of such a garden.

In reality, I would not really want to make each garden room only one color. However, there are many simple ways to combine colors successfully.

COLOR INTENSITY AS A UNIFYING THEME AND OTHER WAYS TO EMPLOY COLOR

Pastels

Our all-pastel garden is tasteful; no one will ever think we are vulgar people, or even passionate ones. Having damned us with faint praise, let me also admit that I have had a soft-color garden for years and it's very pretty, subtle, and easy on the eye. (It's safe, maybe too safe.)

I've seen pastel collections offered in many garden catalogs. The Van Engelen bulb catalog features a pink daffodil and a pink tulip collection. They sound delicious, don't they? In the pastel Asiatic lily collections, the harsh yellows and oranges that are common to Asiatic lilies are eliminated, leaving only shades of cream, white, pink, pale apricot, and the gentlest tones of yellow. Of course, I ordered it for my pastel garden, and I must say it was wonderful, except that two bright-colored bulbs must have rolled in there during packing because a couple of brassy yellow and dark red blooms showed up in June. I cut them to the ground, brought them in the house, and put them in a vase. When the flowers faded in the house, I threw them on the compost heap and that was the end of them.

The truth is, now that we have decided on a pale palate, we have it made. Everything goes with everything. Pale yellow, pale pink, lavender, mauve, cream, apricot, and white get along like peaches and vanilla Häagen-Dazs. We add some true blue flowers to set off pale-colored flowers gorgeously. Plants with blue-green or gray leaves, such as rue (*Ruta graveolens*) and the artemisias are also lovely.

Hot Colors

We are in a tropical garden. *Now* we plant magenta bougainvillea next to taxicab yellow ginger, add red and cerise orchids, then we paint the garden structures chartreuse and turquoise. The only colors I would avoid in a very bright garden are those pale lavenders, peaches, and mauves that look so good in a subtle color scheme. As mentioned in point 8, dusty rose mauve and hot orange mix like pickled herring on vanilla Häagen-Dazs. Nauseating. If you must grow pastel yellow acacias and pink abutilon, keep them on opposite sides of the garden.

Dark Colors

My friend Tracey B. has a mad passion for collecting dark-flowered plants. She thinks they are sexy and brooding, as though they were wearing leather. Her garden is secret and mysterious. That's because you practically have to fall over it to see it. She is crazy about "black" (dark maroon) hollyhocks, pansies, and tulips. She was thrilled when she found a "black" wallflower in an obscure English seed catalog. Plants with dark maroon leaves are also peachy as far as she's concerned. She also collects hellebores, dark roses, deep purple irises, deep purple Chinese tree peonies, and purple lilacs. It is a little Addams Family, frankly, but there is no accounting for such idiosyncrasy. In our garden, we have chosen to combine some of those dark flowers with yellow-leaved shrubs, such as spirea Goldflame, and use yellow privet as a background. We add pale yellow roses and lots of other neutrals and paint the wall cream.

Leaf Color

My friend Mary with the shady garden has become enchanted by leaf color and form. "Enchanted" is not quite the word. "Resigned" is more like it, since the main flowering season in her garden is pretty much kaput by the end of June.

I know many sophisticated gardeners who are much more concerned with the leaves of a plant than its flowers. They say, rightly, that the flowering time of a plant comes and goes, but you have to look at the leaves all season. I am a flower maniac, but even I have to admit the logic of this is inescapable. So it behooves us all to take into consideration leaf form, color, and growth habit when choosing a plant. This is especially true of shrubs, big and permanent as they are.

Odd-colored, striped, dotted, and variegated leaves add variety to an all-green world, but it drives me crazy to see a border composed of nothing but plants with weird-colored leaves. There is a house near the Wal-Mart out on Route 9 whose front yard is graced by a red-leaved Japanese maple (*Acer palmatum*), next to a blue juniper, flanked by a variegated euonymous, underplanted by a gray-leaved rue (*Ruta graveolens*) and silver-leaved artemesia, and a very popular coralbell with coppery red hairy leaves, *Heuchera* 'Palace Purple'. Yecch. What ever happened to green? It reminds me of the women at my mother's hairdresser. They all have ash blond, copper-red, champagne, streaked—everything except gray—hair.

Properly used, however, plants with colorful leaves can be valuable. I like to treat leaf color as though it were flower color, but one that will display itself throughout the season. In my side garden, as I have mentioned, I always had plants with pink, blue, and lavender flowers, but after a couple of years, I wanted to add a touch of yellow to warm it all up. I bought a Goldflame spirea at Charles and Norman's garden exchange for ten dollars and planted it right next to the birdbath in the center of the garden.

It grew into a neat, rounded, three-foot mound of leaves. No, it did not overpower the soft colors. "Goldflame" is a misnomer. The leaves aren't "gold," which I would describe as a shiny yellow-brown metallic substance used as a standard weight in international banking transactions. Nor is it "flame," which I would describe as an orange-red oxidation process. Actually, the leaves of this small shrub are straightforward yellow, which is exactly what I want to complement the pastels.

Unfortunately, this spirea has dinky pink flowers that look like dirty chenille. I have been known to take the hedge shears and lop off the flowers as they appear, thereby giving the plant a shaping at the same time.

In May, it sets off the lavender-violet alliums (*Allium aflatunense*) and blue forget-me-nots (*Myosotis sylvatica*) to perfection. In June, the soft yellow warms up the pink peonies, roses, and multicolored columbines. In July, it complements the blue balloon flowers (*Platycodon*), lavender catnip (*Nepeta mussinii*), *Monarda* 'Mahogany', and pink hollyhocks (*Althaea rosea*). In August, it plays well with creamy yellow daylilies and hot pink phlox. In September, it flatters the purple dahlias and the white Japanese anemone (*Anemone japonica*). And in the fall, it adds another shade of yellow to the general cacophony of leaf color at that time. I liked it so well that a couple of years ago, I took a piece off the side and made two clumps of yellow spireas instead of one. It was fine as long as the shrubs remained small, but as they got bigger and bigger, they took over until everything else began to look like the accompaniment to a pair of four-by-four yellow shrubs. I cut the first one back and pulled the second one out. I never thought I would say this, but you *can* have too much of a good thing.

My friend Peter Bevacqua had a smoke bush (*Cotinus Coggygria*) in his yard when he bought his house. Using the dark purple-red leaf color as a starting point, he found flowers in shades of just the right pink, white, and cream along with a deep maroon that perfectly echos the color of the smoke bush. It's so artistic you could die.

MY COLOR MADNESS

As I've previously indicated, I have a physical reaction to a bad color combination. I used to rip out a hot pink (okay, magenta) perennial sweet pea vine every summer because it clashed with some tiger lilies that had planted themselves in front of it.

Actually, my tiger lilies didn't plant *themselves* in front of the magenta sweet peas in my garden. The truth is, I planted them there. I had taken the little black cormlets from a stand growing in a garden in Brockville, Ontario, when Walter and I were staying at his mother's lake cottage one summer. I had let them drop in my purse "by accident" as we walked by the lily master's front yard. I had forgotten about them until I found them in the bottom of my handbag months after we returned. What was I to do with them—throw them out? I stuck them in the border in front of the sweet pea, figuring they probably wouldn't come up anyway, and even if they did, I could always move them later. Of course, they did come up, and later never came.

Every year I forget to move them and every year the clump gets bigger and bigger. I make a mental note to move them while they are blooming, but by the time they are done, I am busy with the veggie garden and I forget. But does it mean that I'm neurotic because that awful combination upsets me every time I look at it? Am I taking it all too seriously, I ask myself. Have I gone over the edge? Hard to say.

This leads me to:

MY LAST CHRISTOPHER LLOYD STORY

As we strolled the length of his famous long border, Mr. Lloyd called my attention to a clump of orangey-yellow flowers and asked me how I liked the color.

"Bright," I ventured.

"Yes, very bright indeed," he agreed with his authentic English accent.

"Taxi!" I raised my arm as if hailing one. "It's the color of a New York cab," I informed him.

He smiled enigmatically and pointed to some lavender-pink poppies that had seeded themselves among the taxi-colored daisies, a combination that turned the color scheme into a battlefield. "Yes, and what do you think of these two colors together?" he inquired with a slightly naughty twinkle.

"Horrible," I answered honestly, risking insulting my idol.

He wasn't insulted. He laughed. "Oh, but that's why I like it! When you get to be seventy-five, my dear, you don't care if things clash!"

So he was fooling around in the garden! Christopher Lloyd, my hero! He didn't care if his garden met someone else's standards of perfection. He didn't care if it was correct and serious and by the book. Mr. Lloyd had made a garden for his own delight. There's a lesson here, but I won't hit you over the head with it.

When at last—when you are very old perhaps, older than Mr. Lloyd—when at last, years after you began, your yard looks like that drop-dead dream garden of your fantasy, you will have, horticulturally speaking, entered Olympus.

What a happy circumstance. That means your yard is finally finished. You're done. You have nothing more to add or subtract. The fat lady has sung. You never have to work in the garden again.

Ha, ha, ha, you fool. The essential fact of life is not the birds and the bees—not sex, my friend—no, neither is it food nor shelter nor death nor taxes. The essential fact, definition, and condition of life is change. Anyone who has ever gardened will tell you that. You are never finished. Even after the fat lady wraps her tonsils around the last high C, she has to keep weeding, mulching, and cutting back, digging up and replanting between trips to Weight Watchers.

I have done just that, and it has made me the happy woman I am today.

INDEX

*A*bundance planting, 60
Allium, 64, 111
Anchusa, 111
Anemone, 111
Animals:
    protecting gardens from, 30
    See also Deer; Pest protection
Annuals:
    container plants, 147–49
    flowering, 131–32
    self-sowing, 129
Aphids, 162
Arbors:
    rusticated, 42
    as wattle structure, 8, 10
Arches, 40–41, 43
Architectural style:
    arch placement and, 40–41
    cottage gardens and, 2–3
    environment and, 108–9
    fence styles and, 6
    plantings and, 97–109
    tree placement and, 75–77

Aromatic herbs, 111
Art of Beautifying Suburban Home Grounds,
    The, (Scott) xvii
Autumn. *See* Fall
Avent, Tony, 117

*B*acillus thuringiensis, 163
Bat houses, 163
Bayberry, 12
Bee balm, 112
Belvederes, 45
Benign negligence, 125–26
Benner, David, xvi, 185, 186
Berry-bearing shrubs, 12
Bevacqua, Peter, 79
Birdbaths, 51
Black plastic, 157
Bleeding heart, 111
Blue gardens, 177–79
Bluestone Perennials, 119
Books, garden, American vs. British,
    114–16

Borders:
    flower placement, 28–29, 31
    packing, 64–66
    proportion, 83
    red, 180
    shrub, 14–15
    white, 173
Boundaries, 15–16
"Bowling alley" border model, 28–29
Bridal wreath spirea, 72, 113, 141
British gardens:
    advantageous climate, 114–15
    manor house landscaping, 2, 3
    renowned designers, 53–55
    rose growing, 135–38, 174–76
    single-color, 172
Brown cardboard mulch, 157
Bryant Park (New York City), 86
Bulbs, perennial packing, 64–66
Butterfly bush, 129, 145, 159

Cabbage-root maggots, 163
Cardboard:
    as mulch, 157
    in paths, 35
Cargill, Shirley, 135, 137
Carney, Nancy, 69
Carroll Gardens, 117
Carter, Janet, 10
Catalogs, 116–19
    specific, 140, 174, 187
Caterpillars, 163
Catnip, 115
Chain-link fence, 16
Chambers, Anne, 174–76, 179
Chatsworth, England, 2, 3

Chemicals, 161
Chicken wire fencing, 30
Chimney bellflower, 147
Chinese tree peony, 140–41
Chives, 111, 115
Christopher, Thomas, 116
City and Town Gardener, The (Yang), 116
Clematis, 43, 111, 161, 167
Climate, 114–15, 120
Climaxing, 139–45
Cocoa shell mulch, 157
Coconut fiber mulch, 157
Color, 169–91
    blue gardens, 177–79
    dark, 188
    of fences, 16
    gray gardens, 183–85
    green gardens, 185–86
    hot, 187–88
    of leaves, 188–90
    pastels, 187
    red gardens, 179–81
    tips, 169–71
    white gardens, 173–76
    yellow gardens, 181–83
Color in My Garden (Wilder) 181n
Columbine, 111
Compost, 150–53
    making, 152
    mulched weed bundles as, 160
    for packing, 66
    seeds in, 151
    using, 153
Container plants, 147–49
Cotoneaster, 12
Cottage gardens, 1–16
    defined, 1

fences, 5–7
  hedges, 11–14
  shrub borders, 14–15
  straight boundaries, 15–16
  walls, 4–5
Courtyards, 4–5
Cranesbill, 112
Creating a Garden (Keen) 19*n*
Cutworms, 163

Daffodils, 64, 112
Dead plants, 124–25
Deciduous hedges, 12, 13
Deer, 12
  fences against, 30, 110
  plants repellent to, 64, 111–13, 184
Del Lago, Tony, 35–36
Desert gardens, 122–24, 135
Design for Arid Regions (Golny ed.), 109
Deutzia, 12
Digging hole, 166
Diseases, 162
Disney Institute Garden, 90–92
Dividing:
  perennials, 66–68
  shrub suckers, 13, 72
  wildflowers, 120–22
Drift planting:
  perennials, 61–62, 63–64
  shrubs, 71
  trees, 74
Druse, Ken, xv, 115

Eastern-exposure gardens, 99
Elsing Hall, England, rose garden, 135–38

English gardens. *See* British gardens
Evening primrose, 112
Everblooming gardens, 133–67
Evergreen hedges, 12
Evergreens, 144
Exposures, 99–107

Fall (Autumn), 143
Fences, 5–7
  chicken wire, 30
  colors, 16
  proportion formula, 83
  wattle, 7–11
Fertilizer:
  commercial, 163
  in sawdust mulch, 157
Fine Gardening magazine, 69
Firethorn, 12
Flea beetles, 161
Flowering hedges, 13
Flowerpots, 147–49
  outdoor placement, 147–48
  types of, 148–49
Foxglove, 112
Front landscaping, 2–16
  lawn disadvantages, xvi–xviii
Fungus diseases, 162
Fungus gnats, 163
Furniture, garden, 32–34

Garden centers, 119–20
Garden in Autumn, The (Lacy), 115, 121,
  144
Gardening books, 114–16
Garden ornaments, 48–51

Garden rooms, 16–53
    badly placed shrubs, 23–26
    closest to house, 27–28
    flower border placement, 28–29, 31
    layout, 20–23
    paths, 34–39
    seasonal, 146
    seating, 32–34
    second room, 31–32
    themes, 18–20
    third room, 46–48
    tool sheds, 26–27
Garden Variety (television program), 8
Gates, 39–40
Gazebos, 45
Gelman, Michael, 79
Geranium, 112
Globeflower, 112
Globe thistle, 112
Golany, Gideon S. 109*n*
Goldenrod, 142–43
Goldflame spirea, 189
Gooseneck loosestrife, 131
Gophers, 30
Gray gardens, 183–85
Green gardens, 185–86
Green worms, 162
Gustafson, Phyllis, xvi
Gypsy moths, 163

Hall's honeysuckle, 131
Hedges, 11–14
Hemlock, 12
Herbaceous perennials, 62–64, 184
Herbicides, 162, 164
Herbs, aromatic, 111

History of Art (Janson) 57*n*
Hole digging, 166
Holly, 113
Horn worms, 163
Hydrangea, 129, 144, 178

Insects. *See* Pest control
Interval planting, 85–88
Iran, 108, 109
Iris, 112

Janson, H. W., 57*n*
Japanese bamboo, 131
Japanese beetles, 162, 163
Jekyll, Gertrude, 53, 63–64, 67, 146, 178
Joe-pye weed, 121, 122
Johnson, Hugh, 29
Johnson, Ladybird, 52
Johnson, Laurence, 54
Jones, Pamela, 79, 116
Julius II, Pope, 57–58
Just Weeds (Jones), 79, 116

Keen, Lady Mary, 18–20
Kiftsgate Court, England, 174–76
Knotweed, 130–31
Kudzu vine, 131

Lacy, Allen, xvii, 115, 121, 144
Landscaping companies, 119–20
Large yard enclosures, 51
Lavender, 115
Lawns, xvii–xviii

Leaves:
    as color element, 188–90
    as mulch, 156
Live! with Regis and Kathie Lee (television
    show), 88
Lloyd, Christopher, 53–55, 167, 191
Loggias, 44, 45
Loosestrife, 131
Lynch-gate, 43

Manure, 157
Massing, 60–61
McCabe, Sally, 10, 35
Meadow rue, 112
Meadows, 52–55
   artistic vs. unkept, 138
Mexican sunflower, 159
Michelangelo, 57–59
Monet, Claude, 178
Monkshood, 111
Montgomery Place, 128
Moss gardens, 185–86
Mulch, 153–61
    bundled weeds as, 159–61
    newspaper, 69–71, 158
    in paths, 34–35
    wood chips, 153, 154–55
Mulché! See Mulch

National Wildflower Research Center,
    52, 53
Neat gardens, 160–61
Nematodes, 163
Newspaper mulching, 69–71, 158
New York Times Magazine, xvii

Niagara Falls (Canada) public garden,
    88–90
Nitrogen, 156–57
Northern exposure gardens, 100–103
No-Work Garden Book (Stout), 155–56

Oak leaf hydrangea, 129, 144
Onions, ornamental, 111
Organic gardening, 155–56, 163–64
Oriental poppy, 112
Ornaments, garden, 48–51

Packing, 64–66
Page, Russell, 54
Pastel gardens, 187
Paths, 34–39
    laying, 35–39
    proportion formula, 84
Pearly everlasting, 111
Peony, 112, 140–41
Perennials, 56–94
    abundance planting, 60
    dividing, 66–68
    drift planting, 61–62, 63–64
    herbaceous, 62–64
    interval planting, 85–88
    massing, 60–61
    packing, 64–66
    planting proportion formulas, 80–84
    shrubs, 68–74
    between sidewalks and streets, 92–93
    trees, 74–80
Pergolas, 44, 45, 46
Pest control, 161–65
    animal barriers, 30

organic, 163–64
pesticide avoidance, 162
Pesticides, 162
Philadelphia Flower Show, 8
Philadelphia Green, 8, 10
Picket fences, 6
Pine, 12
Plant Delights Nursery, 117
Planting:
    abundance, 60
    compost use, 153
    drift, 61–62, 63–64, 71, 74
    fertilizer, 157, 163
    hole digging, 166
    interval, 85–88
    massing, 60–61
    packing, 64–66
    proportion formulas, 80–84
Plant sales, 126–28
Potentilla, 113, 145
Privet, 11
Proportion, 80–84
Purple loosestrife, 131

Rabbits, 30
Red gardens, 179–81
Root weevils, 163
Rose-of-Sharon, 72, 113, 129, 145
Roses:
    in English gardens, 135–38, 175–76
    June-blooming, 145
    popularity of hybrid teas, 132
    trained over arches, 43, 44
Rotenone, 161
Rousseau, Henri, 60
Russian sage, 113

Sackville-West, Vita, 53–54, 64, 172, 185
Sawdust mulch, 156–57
Scott, Frank J., xvii
Sea lavender, 112
Seasonal garden climaxes, 139–45
Seeds, 151
Self-sowing plants, 128–30
Shade gardens, 101, 111, 112, 185–86
Sheds, storage, 26–27
Shepherd's Seeds, 119, 158
Shrubs, 68–74
    badly placed, 23–26
    in blue gardens, 178
    as borders, 14–15
    deer-resistant, 113
    dividing, 13, 72
    fall-blooming, 144
    fences and, 5
    flowering border, 69–73
    in gray gardens, 184
    as hedges, 11–14
    moving, 26
    perennial interval plantings, 85
    in red gardens, 179–80
    self-sowing, 129
    spring-blooming, 143–44, 145, 183
    summer-blooming, 145
    thinning, 73–74
    trained over arches, 44
    in white gardens, 173
    winter-blooming, 144
Sissinghurst, England, 172
Sistine Chapel, 57–59
Slevin, Ken, 78
Slugs, 163
Snakeroot, 111
Soil, shade garden, 103

Southern-exposure gardens, 105–7
Spades, 166
Spanish walled-front garden, 4
Spider flower, 129
Spirea, 113, 189
Split-rail fences, 6–7
Spring, 143–44, 145
   yellow blooms, 182, 183
Spruce, 12, 113
Stein, Sara, xv
Steinhoff, Tim, 128
Stockade fence, 5
Storage sheds, 26–27
Stout, Ruth, 155–56
Straight lines, 15–16
Straw mulch, 155–56
Suburban landscaping, xvi–xviii, 3–16
Summer, 141–42
   yellow blooms, 182
Sun:
   determining garden design, 108
   protection against, 122–23

Tapestry hedge, 15
Taylor, Norman, 75–76
Taylor's Garden Guide, 75–76
Tea roses, 132
Tent caterpillars, 163
Terra-cotta flowerpots, 148
This Morning with Richard and Judy
   (British television program), 17
Timcah, 108
Tools:
   for dividing, 72
   for hole digging, 166
Tool sheds, 26–27

Trees, 74–80
   arches and, 44
   fences and, 5
   garden rooms and, 21–22, 47
   in gray gardens, 184
   shade, 105
   unwanted, 77–80

Van Engelen catalog, 187
Vegetable garden:
   arches and, 43
   best exposure, 105
   in first garden room, 27
   mulch paths, 35
Verey, Rosemary, 44
Vines:
   in red gardens, 180
   trained over arches, 43
   wattle fences and, 8
Viruses, 162

Walls, 4–5
Water areas, 47, 51
Watering:
   container plants, 148
   desert gardens, 123
   transplants, 13, 162
Water-wise Gardening (Christopher), 116
Wattle fences, 7–11
Weed-barrier mats, 157
Weeding, 165
Weeds:
   bundled as mulch, 159–61
   intentional growing of, 130–31
   wildflowers as, 142

Western-exposure gardens, 104–5
White Flower Farm catalog, 174
White gardens, 145, 173–76
Wilder, Louise Beebe, 181
Wildflowers:
    in cultivated garden, 142
    meadows of, 52–53
    parking lot finds, 120–22
Wild garden, 46–48
Wilting, 162
Winter, 140, 144
Winterthur catalog, 140
Witch hazel, 72, 139–40
Wolfbane, 111

Wood chips:
    as compost, 153, 154–55
    in garden paths, 34–35
Woodchucks, 30
Wooden fences, 5–77
Woodland gardens, 135, 185–86
Wormwood, 111

Yang, Linda, 116
Yarrow, 111
Yellow gardens, 181–83
Yew, 12

ABOUT THE AUTHOR

Lifelong gardener CASSANDRA DANZ is the author of *Mrs. Greenthumbs,* winner of The Garden Writer's Association of America's Quill and Trowel Award, and she writes a regular column for *Country Living Gardener Magazine.* She is also an accomplished comedienne, having appeared in numerous venues, films and TV shows. She lives with her husband and son in New York City and Hudson, New York.